MOVIN' ON UP!

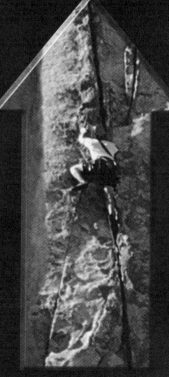

Developing
A Prosperous
Soul For
New Realms
Of Living

by
Marvin Yoder

MOVIN' ON UP!

by
Marvin Yoder

Our Health And Prosperity

The Condition Of Our Soul

Beloved, I wish above all things that thou mayest prosper
and be in health, even as thy soul prospereth.

3 John 2

C·O·N·T·E·N·T·S

Preface

Acknowledgements

Introduction

Endnotes

MOVIN' ON UP!

"*Marvin Yoder has done it again. In his excellent book, **Movin' On Up!**, Marvin helps anyone who is looking to go to the next level.*

*Marvin's book documents the integrity of God's Word, the reality of our redemption and how you and I can be in Christ. Whether a person is dealing with his health, provision, or even his emotions, **Movin' On Up!** is a step-by-step blueprint for going to the next level.*

Marvin Yoder is a man with a mission. His writing is motivational and his methods are founded in Bible-based character and integrity. I strongly recommend this book for anyone desiring to grow in the Christian life."

Van Crouch
Motivational Speaker
President, Van Crouch Communications

P·R·E·F·A·C·E

The information in this book has the potential to help change your life! When you start on the journey toward a prosperous soul, your life will begin to change dramatically. Things in your life that you have not dealt with may confront you. You may finally be able to move toward the dream you've had for so long. You may suddenly realize that your God-given potential and destiny is possible, and that it can come to pass.

The most important thing you can do as you look at the principles contained in this book is to be totally honest with yourself. God will help you as you are truthful about the condition of your soul. Sometimes it hurts to find out we're not as far along as we thought in life. But just be honest with God and yourself about the condition of your soul, and it will be possible for you to experience the growth you desire.

Don't give up as you develop a prosperous soul. Realize that you didn't get into the condition you're in overnight; God will lead you step by step in the direction of developing a prosperous soul. Developing a prosperous soul is a daily process – not just a one-time event. Be encouraged that you **can** receive increase in your life, and move on up to the level God wants for you as you persist in applying Biblical principles into your life.

A·C·K·N·O·W·L·E·D·G·E·M·E·N·T·S

To my wife, Leah, who stands by
me in the ministry faithfully and
encourages me to do what God is
telling me to do.

To my children, Christina, Nichole,
and Audrey, who have allowed me
to obey God and work many hours
to complete this project.

To Pastor Greg Roe, for recognizing
my writing abilities.

To Pastor Scott Porter, for
proofreading my manuscript.

To Mr. Van Crouch, for giving me
many ideas for this book.

To Creative Images for their
insight, wisdom, and help in
printing this book.

Front Cover Photo: Chris Rebman

Thank you all for your
encouragement and help.

I·N·T·R·O·D·U·C·T·I·O·N

I'll never forget the first day I ventured out on a mountain in the Rockies. I had been up in the Appalachian Mountains, the Smokey Mountains, and had even gone mountain climbing in Eastern Europe. But let me tell you, you've never really seen a mountain until you've seen the Rocky Mountains, because they're much bigger and taller than most other mountain ranges!

When I stood atop one of the Rocky Mountains for the first time, I was higher up than I had ever been before with my feet still on the ground. At first, I was frightened and overwhelmed. Feelings of fear rose up in me because it appeared that if I ever fell, I wouldn't stop falling for a half mile or more. I felt out of control, unable to function, and I was unfamiliar with the environment at that level.

I began to understand why many people don't want to move up in life. Being up this high required change in the way a person did things. Overcoming fear of new heights, adjustment to an unfamiliar environment, and learning different principles and rules in which to operate are all a part of entering new realms. It is obvious that when you are at a higher altitude, whether on a mountain or in real life, what worked on a lower level will not work there.

After that first day up on the mountain, I went back to my motel room, feeling as though I never wanted to see another mountain the rest of my life! However, the next day I decided to spend the whole day in the mountains, because I did not want fear, feelings of intimidation, or any other negative experiences to govern how I would function in the future. After being at a higher altitude for a period of time and becoming a little more familiar with the environment and the rules of operation there, I actually began to enjoy it.

I saw a perspective in looking at things that I had never been able to see before. It's a different world when you move up to a higher level. Life can be unbelievably beautiful, uncluttered, pure, and uncomplicated when you are up higher. There is nothing like being elevated where you're able to see the big picture!

This book will help you get a perspective of moving on up to a new level of living. What is presented here is based upon the Word of God. *The key to moving up higher in life is developing a prosperous soul that will embrace in thought and principle where you want to go in life.*

Chapter 1
A PROSPEROUS SOUL

Several years ago there was a popular TV program with a theme song entitled, *"Movin' on up..."* That's what this book is all about. God wants you to move on up to what He promised you in His Word. *God wants you to know that today is not a life sentence!* He wants to help you break into new realms of living, prosperity, and health. Get ready to move on up to a new realm of living you've never experienced before!

A PROSPEROUS SOUL

Beloved, I wish above all things that thou mayest prosper and be in health, even as thy soul prospereth.
(3 John 2)

In this verse God tells us He wants, above all else, that two things would happen to His children. He wants us to (1) prosper, and (2) have good health. God is discussing a matter of importance, or priority here in **3 John 2**, so we need to pay attention to what He is saying. If it is important to God, it should also be important to us. When we have the same priorities God has, we can have what He has promised us in His Word.

The Apostle John may not have realized the significance of the greeting he penned in his letter to Gaius that we know as **3 John 2**. However, it expressed the Father's will for His children so accurately that He declared this is His Word for His children. **3 John** may have started as a letter from one man to another, but when God included this letter in the Holy Scriptures, it became a part of the infallible Word of God that lives and prevails forever! It is God speaking to you today!

If **John 3:16** is for you today then **3 John 2** is also for you today! **2 Timothy 3:16** declares that *"ALL SCRIPTURE is given by inspiration of God, and IS PROFITABLE for doctrine, for reproof, for correction, for instruction in righteousness:"*

3 John 2 is expressing the will of God for your life, which includes prosperity and health. Just as **John 3:16** declares God's will to all sinners, **3 John 2** declares God's will to all Christians. It is up to you to decide what you want.

PROSPERITY AND HEALTH ARE THE WILL OF GOD FOR YOU

Prosperity includes your spiritual progress, family well-being, and success in your finances, ministry, and your employment. It also has to do with your obedience to God. Prosperity really includes whatever you are involved in. There is more to it than just money.

The Greek word for "prospereth" is *eudoo*. Vine's Expository Dictionary states that *"in this verse it is used in the continuing sense, suggesting the successive circumstances of varying prosperity as week follows week."* Strong's Exhaustive Concordance further defines this word as meaning *to help on the road, to succeed in reaching, fig. to succeed in business affairs.*

Health includes your physical well-being, your mental and emotional state, your strength and energy and so forth. Your health includes all areas of your being: spirit, soul, and body. Every area of your life is affected by the condition of your soul.

Why are your prosperity and health so important to God? *They're important because God knows that when you are prosperous and healthy you are in the best possible position to obey Him.*

Isn't salvation more important than prosperity and health? It is true that if a person is not born again, then salvation is more important. However, since this verse is written to Christians, it reveals that in fulfilling the will of God, two very important issues for us to deal with are prosperity and health.

Poor people may have a desire to obey God but they lack the resources to do so. Sick people may want to serve God, but they are physically unable to do so. God is not against a person because he is poor or sick. He has provided the answer for poverty and sickness, and He wants to help people move out of the things that keep them bound. God wants His people free so they can do what He tells them to do.

Some people have the mistaken idea that their sickness or poverty enables them to be witnesses for Christ in the earth. Perhaps in the midst of these conditions these people do have opportunities to share their faith with others. But how much more could they do if they were free from sickness and poverty, and had the physical ability and the resources to obey whatever God told them to do? When you have the prosperity and health God has promised in His Word, you are able to accomplish much more for the Kingdom of God.

GOD'S WILL IS NOT AUTOMATIC

Notice that while God's will for you is prosperity and health, it is not automatic. There are conditions to be met. Jack Hartman said, *"Of course our Father wants us to be successful, healthy, and prosperous, but did you notice the five-word 'qualifier' at the end – 'even as thy soul prospereth?'*

These last five words are the cause of the prosperity and health that our Father wants so much for us."[1]

Gloria Copeland wrote in her book GOD'S WILL IS PROSPERITY, *"...you will prosper to the degree that your soul prospers. Bible prosperity will not come any other way. The laws of prosperity are based upon obedience to God's Word. That is the built-in protection of prosperity."*[2]

This is why state lotteries are not ordained of God. They award large sums of money to individuals on the basis of a winning ticket instead of having a prosperous soul. Many people who have won state lotteries now have ruined lives because they received great increase which exceeded the condition of their souls. They made poor decisions about their money and spent it on things that were detrimental to their well-being, or they lost it in some way. This is what happens when the equation in **3 John 2** is out of balance.

Proverbs 10:22 tells us that *"**The blessing of the Lord, it maketh rich, and he addeth no sorrow with it.**"* In other words, God will not bless you beyond the level of what your soul can handle. T.D. Jakes said, *"It is a spiritual progression of events that Christians should prosper and be in good health even as our souls prosper. The same God who causes us to prosper spiritually causes us to prosper physically and financially. The concept is 'as your soul' which literally means in proportion."*[3]

Look at **3 John 2** again. *"**Beloved, I wish above all things that thou mayest prosper and be in health, even as thy soul prospereth.**"* In this verse, John indicates a relationship between the condition of a person's soul and his prosperity and health. He said our prosperity and health is "even as" our soul prospers; not "more than" or "less than." If I were a mathematician, I would state this relationship in the form of an equation which would look like this:

4

YOUR PROSPERITY & HEALTH ARE EQUAL TO THE CONDITION OF YOUR SOUL

An equation has two equal sides. If one part is changed, the equalities are no longer true. Most of the promises in God's Word have a "God side" and a "man side" which must be completed in order for that promise to manifest in your life. Therefore, if you change "the condition of the soul" side in this equation, God will change the "prosperity and health" side. Several truths can be learned from this equation.

First of all, your health and prosperity are governed by the condition of your soul. It is impossible for your health and prosperity to exceed the condition of your soul.

Secondly, you may know the will of God for your life, but the condition of your soul will determine what you experience in life. It is true that God said in His Word that all of His promises are for you, but the condition of your soul will actually determine if you experience those promises.

Thirdly, you can know a truth in your spirit, but if you're not convinced of it in your soul, you will not operate in it because the decisions of life are made in the soul.

Knowing this equation takes the mystery out of obtaining the prosperity, health, and increase that God wants you to have. You can start on the road to God's will for your life any time you choose by changing the condition of your soul. You start by changing your thinking. The power to change your soul is within your reach by reading the Word of God and with the help of the Holy Spirit. Today can be the first day of changing the condition of your soul, and experiencing new levels of living.

Your real problem is not your boss, your parents, your environment, or your upbringing. Your greatest problem is between your two ears! The good news is that since your problem is the condition of your soul, you can do something about it! Your problem is not beyond your reach. You don't have to stay the same; you can start changing the condition of your soul whenever you want.

We are not talking about things beyond a person's control. For example, a person has no control over his upbringing, the environment in which he grew up, or the decisions made by his parents. Accidents happen to people, and trouble is no respecter of persons.

However, possessing a prosperous soul will enable you to respond in a scriptural manner when these things happen to you, and God will have the last word in your situation. You may not have been in control of your past, but you can take charge of your future by developing a prosperous soul so that the will of God comes to pass in your life.

THE IMPORTANCE OF A PROSPEROUS SOUL

Your prosperity, health, and experiences in life can be determined and measured by the condition of your soul. The soul becomes the key to your spiritual, mental, physical, financial, and social progress in life because that is where the decisions of life are made. This effects every area of your life.

As you pursue God and attempt to move up into the increase and realms of living He has promised you in His Word, there are several things you need to keep in mind. There is the aspect of simply knowing who God is, and what He has for you. Another aspect is the law of sowing and reaping. Yet another aspect to obtaining God's increase is faith in His Word. Also, the anointing and the miraculous power of the Holy Spirit play a part in receiving increase. However, unless you develop a prosperous soul, all these other aspects of obtaining increase from God will be difficult to operate and maintain. Right thinking is a prerequisite and a priority if you are going to successfully function in these other areas of increase and move up to new realms of living.

Notice what John wrote in **3 John 3,** *"For I rejoiced greatly, when the brethren came and testified of the truth that is in thee, even as thou walkest in the truth."* In verse two John states the necessity of a prosperous soul. In verse three John said he rejoiced greatly when he heard that his fellow Christians had the truth, or the Word of God in them. This reveals that having a prosperous soul and having the truth in you are synonymous. Apart from having the Word of God in you, it is impossible to have a prosperous soul.

A prosperous soul is one with the Word of God in it. Anything else would be less than what God wants. You can know you have the truth in you when it shows up in your lifestyle, who you associate with, the places you go, your countenance, and your attitudes. When the Word of God becomes a part of your soul, change takes place in your life.

YOUR HEALTH AND WELL-BEING

The condition of your soul affects your health and well-being. John G. Lake said, *"...the condition of the body will be a revelation of the attitude of the mind."*[4] Some of the medical field is acknowledging what the Bible says about our physical health being related to the condition of our souls. Dr. S. I. McMillan wrote in his book NONE OF THESE DISEASES, *"...medical science recognizes that emotions such as fear, sorrow, envy, resentment, and hatred are responsible for the majority of our sicknesses. Estimates vary from 60% to nearly 100%."*[5]

Proverbs 17:22 says, *"A merry heart doeth good like a medicine: but a broken spirit drieth the bones."*

Proverbs 4:20-23 also tells us, *"My son, attend unto my words; incline thine ear unto my sayings. Let them not depart from thine eyes; keep them in the midst of thine heart. For they are life unto those that find them, and health to all their flesh."* These verses reveal that the condition of your soul has an affect upon your physical body.

YOUR ACHIEVEMENTS AND DESTINY

The condition of your soul has an effect upon your achievements and your ultimate destiny in life. Ralph Waldo Emerson declared, *"A man is what he thinks about all day long."*[6] Norman Vincent Peale stated that if you *"Change your thoughts... you change your world."*[7] John Osteen said, *"You create the atmosphere in which you live by the thoughts you entertain for constant meditation. Thoughts are like the seeds in trees and flowers. When they are planted, they will 'bring forth after their kind.'"*[8] Look at **Genesis 1:11-12** to understand the principle of seedtime and harvest, then apply it to your thought life.

What you allow into your soul and store there will determine what kind of person you become. You are a product of the thoughts you think continually, the imaginations you entertain, and what you choose to remember of the past. You must choose carefully what you bring into your mind.

In 1954, Roger Bannister was the first person to run an officially recorded four-minute mile.[9] Prior to that event some schools taught that it was a physical impossibility for the human body to withstand the pressures of running a four-minute mile. Did the human race undergo a change in physical anatomy in 1954? No, in reality Roger Bannister didn't so much break a physical barrier or a time barrier as he broke a "mind barrier."

After Roger Bannister ran the four-minute mile in 1954, thirty-seven people did it in 1955, and over three hundred people ran a four-minute mile in 1956. Recently a high school boy ran a four-minute mile, but he received no honor or prize because he finished in eighth place! Roger Bannister changed the whole world of track and running forever because he entertained thoughts that he could run a four-minute mile!

You are never so powerful as when you decide what kind of information you allow into your mind. Your destiny is decided by a thought, an imagination, an idea, or a memory that you choose to dwell upon. Your greatest limitations in life are not your parents, your upbringing, or your environment. The highest hurdles you will jump and the greatest battles you will fight are in your soul as you endeavor to obey God. John Maxwell stated that, *"You are where you are and what you are because of the dominating thoughts that occupy your mind ...most intelligent people never move beyond the boundaries of their self-imposed limitations."*[10]

YOUR FINANCIAL PROSPERITY

The condition of your soul will affect your financial and business success. In his book SEE YOU AT THE TOP, Zig Ziglar wrote, *"A study by Harvard University revealed that 85% of the reasons for success, accomplishments, promotions, etc., were because of our attitudes and only 15% because of our technical expertise."*

Your success and promotion may depend more upon your attitude toward the company than in your ability to do the work. Even if you don't qualify for the "technical expertise" line to promotion, you can still qualify by being in the "attitude" line. So keep on believing that, *If God be for us who can be against us?"* (Romans 8:31).

Your soul must change if you want your prosperity and health to change. Begin to embrace new thoughts from God's Word.

Enlarge your mind so you can embrace what God tells you to do. Some people resist change. They're like concrete: thoroughly mixed up and absolutely set!

Bob Harrison stated, *"You will never change until you are willing to spend money to change your mind."*[12] What did he mean? Be willing to spend money to go to school, buy books, audio tapes, and video tapes and begin to feed on them. The information you receive from them will change your soul. He went on to say, *"Some people spend more money on their cars than they do on their minds. That is why their cars run better than their minds do!"*[12]

Let your mind be stretched to embrace new ideas. Think larger thoughts than you ever dared to think before. Dream your dreams until they are so big that the only way they can come to pass is if God does it by His Spirit!

Oliver Wendall Holmes said, *"A man's mind stretched to a new idea never goes back to its original dimensions"*[13] A person's whole life is governed by how his soul functions. Destinies are decided many years before the actual events occur because of the thoughts, ideas, imaginations, and memories that are allowed to dwell in the soul. ***"For as he thinks in his soul, so is he ..."*** (Proverbs 23:7, ABPS).

POINTS TO PONDER

1. THE DECISIONS OF LIFE ARE MADE IN THE SOUL.

2. OUR PROSPERITY AND HEALTH ARE EQUAL TO THE CONDITION OF OUR SOUL.

3. DESTINIES ARE DECIDED MANY YEARS BEFORE THE ACTUAL EVENTS OCCUR BECAUSE OF THE THOUGHTS, IDEAS, IMAGINATIONS, AND MEMORIES THAT ARE ALLOWED TO DWELL IN THE SOUL.

Chapter 2
DEFINING THE SOUL

Man is made up of three basic parts: spirit, soul, and body. The soul in the Greek is called *psuche*, referring to *the inward man (spirit), or the seat of the new life*, according to Vine's Expository Dictionary.

Some people do not recognize a difference between the soul and the spirit. However, according to the Word of God they are not the same. Notice in the following scriptures the soul and spirit are mentioned separately, as two distinct parts of a human being.

And the very God of peace sanctify you wholly; and I pray God your whole spirit and soul and body be preserved blameless unto the coming of our Lord Jesus Christ.
(1 Thessalonians 5:23)

For the word of God is quick, and powerful, and sharper than any twoedged sword, piercing even to the dividing asunder of soul and spirit, and of the joints and marrow, and is a discerner of the thoughts and intents of the heart.
(Hebrews 4:12)

The word "soul" is used several ways in the Word of God. Sometimes it refers to the whole being of man, such as in **Acts 2:43, "And fear came upon every soul: and many wonders and signs were done by the apostles."** It also may refer to certain people or a group of people, i.e. **1 Peter 3:20, "...God waited in the days of Noah, while the ark was a preparing, wherein few, that is, eight souls were saved by water."** In this book, the soul is referred to as a part of the makeup of man, as **Psalms 23:3** tells us, *"He restoreth my soul: he leadeth me in the paths of righteousness for his name's sake."*

The soul is made up of three basic parts: the mind, the will, and the emotions. Other parts of the soul exist, but our studies will concentrate primarily on these three basic parts.

God wants our minds to be transformed by His Word, our wills to be conformed to His will, and our emotions to be stabilized so we can freely follow His leading. These things will be defined in greater depth in later chapters. Dr. Jerry Savelle said, *"A prosperous soul is one in which the mind is renewed, the will conformed, the emotions controlled, and the thinking faculties selective of that which it thinks."*[1]

You must understand what the purpose and function of the soul and its various parts are so you can cooperate with them and have the best God has for you. Because of simple lack of knowledge, or misunderstanding, many people are living lives that are unfulfilled and filled with frustration. They are living far below the level of God's will and promises. Only when we understand what goes on in our souls and begin to operate the principles of God's Word concerning the soul, can we maximize our relationship with God, and move up to the level of living God wants us to have.

Psalms 1:1 reads, *"Blessed is the man that walketh not in the counsel of the ungodly ... "* The Word of God states that a person is blessed by God when he gets the right kind of help. What is the right kind of help? The Holy Spirit will help you in your soul according to the Word of God. This means when you need counseling, find someone who believes the Word of God and is led by the Holy Spirit to counsel you. Then you will make your way prosperous and be successful.

Dr. Jerry Savelle said in his book PROSPERITY OF THE SOUL, *"Prosperity of the soul comes when one walks in truth, and follows that which is good. You cannot prosper in the soulish realm without the aid of God's Word. You must walk in truth: walk in the counsel of God."*[2] We're not talking about just using your will power and strength to change yourself. You must incorporate the Word of God as the foundation for any positive, lasting change in your soul.

As a Christian, you are not to rely upon the world for help with your soul. The best help the world can offer is temporary. Rush Limbaugh coined the phrase *"psycho-babble,"* referring to *intellectual talk that is unable to change anything.* Often, what the world tells you may sound good, but it contains no real substance that can help a person change permanently. Many times all they can tell you is the problem, but not the answer.

A friend of mine was having some problems, so he went to a psychologist for help. After spending numerous sessions with the psychologist, at fifty dollars an hour, the psychologist told my friend what his problem was. As my friend told me later, "I already knew what my problems were. What I needed was answers to those problems!"

GOD WANTS YOUR SOUL
TO DWELL IN PEACE

And the peace of God, which passeth all understanding, shall keep your hearts and minds through Christ Jesus.
(Philippians 4:7)

Often, the condition of our soul is determined by our circumstances, environment, relatives, childhood upbringing, level of social status, or degree of education. However, if these things affect the soul until we live our lives in the light of them, we will be far below the level on which God wants us to live.

The great battles of life often take place in the soul of man. Spiritual warfare in the soulish arena, via your thoughts, imaginations, and attitudes either from the Word of God or Satan, often decide the outcome of your life. Satan tries to rob you of your peace of mind so you can't flow with the will of God for your life. God sent His Word so you could walk according to His will and experience peace of mind. If you can win the battle in your mind, the battles in the heavenlies will be no problem.

As your soul is renewed by the Word of God, you will become selective of the thoughts that you dwell upon; therefore you will experience the peace of God. The more you renew your soul to the Word of God, the greater God's peace will be in your life. **Psalms 119:165** reveals that, *"Great peace have they which love thy law: and nothing shall offend them."*

When someone tells you he has no peace of mind, usually the real problem can be found by looking at what he is putting in his mind. He has not constantly, on a regular basis, put the Word of God in his mind and heart until the promises of God's Word gives him assurance that everything will be all right, and God will take care of him. The level of peace in your mind depends upon the level that you receive from the promises of God's Word.

1 Thessalonians 5:23 states that, *"And the very God of peace sanctify you wholly; and I pray God your whole spirit and soul and body be preserved blameless unto the coming of our Lord Jesus Christ."* This verse reveals the value of the peace of God. *We could say it this way: the peace of God will preserve your whole being; spirit, soul, and body.*

The prosperity of your soul is directly related to the peace of God. St. Augustine said it this way, *"My soul is restless until it finds rest in thee, O God."*[3] In other words, his soul had no rest until it found the peace of God.

The peace of God will preserve your soul even in the midst of trying times. In the midst of great personal tragedy, when he lost his whole family, Horatio P. Spafford penned the words to the great hymn that is still sung today:

> *When peace like a river attendeth my way,*
> *When sorrows like sea billows roll,*
> *Whatever my lot, thou hast taught me to say,*
> *It is well, it is well with my soul.*[4]

God is faithful to take care of you as you make sure your soul is prospering in the Word of God. The great American poet, John Greenleaf Whittier, must have had a revelation of obtaining the peace of God as he wrote, *"Take from our souls the strain and stress, And let our ordered lives confess – the beauty of thy peace."*[5] The peace of God becomes vital to the well-being of our souls.

MAINTAINING PEACE IN YOUR MIND

The way to maintain peace of mind is to choose your thoughts. What you choose to continually think about will ultimately determine the condition of your soul. This is why **Philippians 4:8** tells you what to think on.

> *Finally, brethren, whatsoever things are true, whatsoever things are honest, whatsoever things are just, whatsoever things are pure, whatsoever things are lovely, whatsoever things are of good report; if there be any virtue, and if there be any praise, think on these things.*
> **(Philippians 4:8)**

There are things that are true, but they are not lovely, nor do they have a good report. There are things that are honest, but there is neither praise nor virtue (admirable quality, merit, or moral excellence) exhibited in them.

For example, it may be a true and honest report that the crime rate among America's teenagers is higher than it was thirty years ago, but this is not a good report, nor a lovely situation. It has no praise or virtue in it. Therefore, dwelling continually upon that report, especially if you have a teenager or are about to have one, can cause you to become fearful and lose your peace of mind.

BUILDING CASTLES IN YOUR SOUL

(For the weapons of our warfare are not carnal, but mighty through God to the pulling down of strong holds;) Casting down imaginations, and every high thing that exalts itself against the knowledge of God, and bringing into captivity every thought to the obedience of Christ.
(2 Corinthians 10:4-5)

A process occurs in your soul in which thoughts you continually dwell upon lead to imaginations, and as you continue to imagine those thoughts, eventually they become strongholds in your soul. If your thoughts go unchecked, this process produces negative results. You can purposefully focus your thoughts and imaginations in the direction of God's Word and His will for you until they become strongholds in your soul.

Imaginations are simply images we allow to play in our minds. The Scribner-Bantam English Dictionary defines imaginations as *"the ability to create ideas or images independent of the external world. It presents images characterized by grandeur of conception, exaltation of mood, and that piercing vision which detects truth. The scientist, the poet, the wise parent, the great teacher, alike exercise it."*[6]

Depending upon what images you allow to occupy your mind during the process of imagination, you will either be lifted up into the peace God has given to you, or you will find yourself living far below the lifestyle He intended for you. If you dwell upon these images long enough, they will become etched in your soul until they become strongholds in your mind and in your life.

What is a stronghold in your soul? The Greek meaning of the word "stronghold" in the verse above refers to *a fortification, or fortress, or to hold safely a castle.* Attitudes and habitual thought patterns are the castles you build in your soul. This is why your attitudes and thought patterns seem so impregnable and totally fortified until they look like they cannot be changed. They have become strongholds in your soul.

Attitudes emerge from imaginations entertained, and imaginations are thoughts dwelled upon. Thought is the seed of attitudes, and imaginations are the soil in which attitudes grow. John Dryden said, *"We first make our habits, and then our habits make us."*[7]

You may find yourself trying to change old attitudes yet expressing the same attitudes you always did before. How do you tear down an attitude that is a fortress or castle in your soul? The answer is found in the way it is built.

A castle is built one stone at a time. Stones become walls, and walls become castles. In the same way, your attitudes are built one thought at a time. If you want to tear down old attitudes and build new ones in your soul, you must do it one thought at a time. Remember, the process starts with a thought, becomes an imagination, and eventually forms a stronghold in your soul.

For example, no one decided on the spur of the moment that he was going to commit an act of adultery. Such an act is the product of thoughts unchecked in a person's mind until he imagines the event in his mind. After awhile, these thoughts become a stronghold in the mind, and that person commits the actual event. Ralph Waldo Emerson said, *"the ancestor of every action is a thought ...thought is the seed of action."*[8]

You can change any attitude or thought pattern you have by understanding this process. The thoughts of the Word of God can form the attitudes and thought patterns in your soul until you have a soul that is a fortress of peace. Changing the condition of your soul will cause you to experience a new life you never had before!

The soul is changed, either for good or bad, through a process over a period of time. Every thought, imagination, idea, or memory is important because it can either add to or take away from your peace of mind, your relationship with God, and your moving up to where God wants you to live.

POINTS TO PONDER

1. THE MIND IS TO BE RENEWED BY THE WORD OF GOD, THE WILL IS TO BE CONFORMED TO GOD'S WILL, AND THE EMOTIONS ARE TO BE STABILIZED SO YOU CAN FREELY FOLLOW GOD'S LEADING.

2. YOU MUST INCORPORATE THE WORD OF GOD AS THE FOUNDATION FOR ANY POSITIVE, LASTING CHANGE IN YOUR SOUL.

3. GOD'S ORIGINAL INTENTION WAS FOR MAN'S SOUL TO DWELL IN PEACE.

4. THE THOUGHTS OF THE WORD OF GOD CAN FORM THE ATTITUDES AND THOUGHT PATTERNS IN YOUR SOUL UNTIL YOU HAVE A SOUL THAT IS A FORTRESS OF PEACE.

Chapter 3

UNDERSTANDING THE MIND

We're learning how to develop a prosperous soul so we can move to new levels of living. This chapter looks at a part of the soul called the mind to see how it functions, and how you can learn to make good decisions in life.

MANY KINDS OF MINDS ARE MENTIONED IN THE BIBLE

The Word of God mentions people with carnal, or fleshly minds (Romans 8:6,7, Colossians 2:18), reprobate minds (Romans 1:28), corrupt minds (1 Timothy 6:5, 2 Timothy 3:8), doubtful minds (Luke 12:29), despiteful minds (Ezekiel 36:5), and those who are double minded (James 1:8, 4:8).

On the other hand, the Word of God instructs believers to be sober minded (Titus 2:6), have a lowly or humble mind (Acts 20:19, Philippians 2:3, Colossians 3:12), have a willing or ready mind (Acts 17:11, 2 Corinthians 8:12, 1 Peter 5:2), and to be pure minded (2 Peter 3:1). God gives believers a sound mind (2 Timothy 1:7), and believers are to have spiritual minds, or the mind of Christ (Romans 8:6,27; 12:2, 1 Corinthians 2:16).

Recognizing all these different kinds of minds mentioned here enables us to understand why trouble abounds in the world. All these different kinds of minds are the products of the thoughts that people have entertained. Therefore their minds think differently, have different values and beliefs, and have different goals. Their likes and dislikes aren't the same, so disagreements and arguments often take place.

Have you ever stopped to think how many different kinds of minds are present in just one roomful of people? This is one reason why disagreements and difficulties take place in families and organizations, including churches. It is important that people " ...*be perfectly joined together in the same mind and in the same judgment*" (1 Corinthians 1:10). Being of the same mind enables people to have the same judgment, reach the same conclusion, and take the same course of action.

UNDERSTANDING THE MIND

The mind is where information is stored. It remembers all that has ever happened to you. It also assimilates thoughts and imaginations. The information in the mind causes your human will to either submit or rebel, and governs your emotions and feelings.

The mind is like a tape player, which basically does two things. It records new information, and it plays back what is recorded.

You can choose which function is activated. Too many times people simply play recorded information (remembering past things) instead of recording new material to replace the old (gathering new information via their thoughts and imaginations).

The information brought into your mind and stored there determines what kind of person you become. **Proverbs 23:7** states that *"...as he thinketh in his heart, so is he."* James Allen said, *"A man is literally what he thinks, his character being the complete sum of all his thoughts."*[1] You are a product of the thoughts you think continually, the imaginations you entertain, and the memories of the past that you choose to remember. Dr. Lester Sumrall wrote in his book OVERCOMING COMPULSIVE DESIRES, *"Believe me, there is no such thing as an idle thought. We are what we think. Nothing reveals our true selves as much as the things we allow our minds to dwell on habitually. And those thoughts inevitably show up in our attitudes, our words, and our actions."*[2]

This reminds me of a poem I read recently about the mind:

"The mind is a garden that can be cultivated to produce the harvest we desire.

The mind is a workshop where the important decisions of life and eternity are made.

The mind is the armory where we forge the weapons for our victory or our destruction.

The mind is a battlefield where all the decisive battles of life are won or lost."
(Unknown)

You must choose carefully what you bring into your mind. You are never so powerful as when you choose what kind of information you allow into your mind, because your destiny is decided by a thought, an imagination, an idea, or a memory that you dwell upon.

Victor E. Frankl was an Austrian psychotherapist who was imprisoned in Nazi concentration camps from 1942 to 1945 during the Holocaust in World War II. After his release he said, *"the last of the human freedoms – to choose one's attitude in any given set of circumstances."*[3] If anyone were ever qualified to make a statement like that, it would be a person who underwent such atrocities and negative circumstances, and survived. In fact, choosing your attitudes in the midst of trying times is a real key to surviving the ordeal you are going through.

HOW THE MIND GATHERS INFORMATION

The mind is affected or changed through a process and not instantaneously like the human spirit is. The work of God is a process in your mind. Your mind grows in God, in His Word, and in His grace to walk in His will through applying the Word daily.

The mind gathers information through two ways (1) the conscience (2) the five physical senses.

The mind receives information through the conscience, from the human spirit, where the Holy Spirit resides. The conscience brings knowledge from the spirit realm, speaks the will of God, and will function according to the Word of God.

The five physical senses bring information from the physical body and the physical world.

For example, the sense of touch sends a message to your mind that the stove is hot and the mind then makes a decision that you should stop touching the stove. The sense of taste tells the mind a certain food tastes good and the mind then decides it wants more. When the physical body experiences pain, it sends a message to the mind that something needs to be done about it.

The world appeals to the sense of sight and hearing to send information to your mind. It is trying to influence your thinking, either to gain your support or to desensitize you toward a particular issue or product. Businesses utilize the sense of sight to sell their products, displaying them in newspapers, television, and on billboards.

The sense of sight sends the strongest messages from the physical realm to the mind. People are moved by what they see. For example, if you put green food coloring on a perfectly cooked steak, no one will want to eat it, even though there is nothing harmful in it. This is why television has become such an effective medium to convey information in our society. The things people see move them to think certain thoughts, go in a particular direction, or do specific things. Even the devil tries to get people to see certain things in order to cause them to respond in a certain way.

And be not conformed to this world: but be ye transformed by the renewing of your mind, that ye may prove what is that good, and acceptable, and perfect will of God.

(Romans 12:2)

The mind gathers information continuously, and updates its "information files" as new information is received. This brings out the value of daily devotions in the Word of God. As you renew your mind, you are deleting the information files of the world, and creating new information files in your mind according to the Word of God.

Therefore if any man be in Christ, he is a new creature: old things are passed away; behold, all things are become new.

(2 Corinthians 5:17)

Spiritual things can change instantly, as in salvation, or a miracle. When a person becomes born again, his human spirit is instantly recreated. A brand new "inner man" has come into being according to **2 Corinthians 5:17**. Faster than you can blink your eye, the power of God removes the human spirit with its old sin nature and puts within you a spirit of righteousness!

However, soulish things change through a process, and it takes time. This is why you need to hear the same information over and over again. The mind is not recreated like your spirit is when you are born again. Your mind is designed to be renewed day by day until your thought patterns reflect the plan of God for your life and level of life God wants you to live.

Taking Care Of Your Mind

You must learn to take care of your mind. You cannot put trashy material in your mind and think great, positive, and powerful thoughts in a crisis, or when under pressure. Your mind is sensitive to every piece of information it receives, either from the spirit realm or from this world.

Helen McInnes wrote in the preface of her book entitled HORIZONS, *"The mind is more vulnerable than the stomach because it can be poisoned without feeling immediate pain."*[4] How can your mind be poisoned? – By the attitudes you harbor in your soul.

For example, doubt is an attitude that will poison your soul. It eats away at your confidence and your courage. Alexander Dumas said, *"A person who doubts himself is like a man who enlists in the ranks of his enemy and gears arms against himself."*[5] Doubt will undermine your ability to trust in God, His Word, and in yourself.

You must believe in yourself – if you don't, nobody else will. Boost your self-esteem by seeing what God has to say in His Word about you. Begin to consciously think thoughts you find in God's Word. You can choose what thoughts you think about yourself. *"Our best friends and our worst enemies are the thoughts we think about ourselves."*[6] (Dr. Frank Crane).

Booker T. Washington said, *"I will permit no man to narrow and degrade my soul by making me hate him."*[7] Allowing things like hate, fear, bitterness, and unforgiveness in your life will poison your mind. *"The human mind is like the human body. It can be wounded. Sorrow is a wound. It cuts deeply, but sorrow is a clean wound, and will heal unless something gets into the wound, such as bitterness, self-pity, or resentment."*[8] (Charles L. Allen).

Each person will at some point in his lifetime experience wounds in his soul. However, it is the choice of each person whether he allows his soul to become poisoned with thoughts and attitudes as a result of those wounds.

Mike Murdock said, *"Refuse the chains of past injustices ... Injustice is only as powerful as the memory of it."*[9] Often people continue to poison their minds by holding on to the memory of things that happened in the past. Let go of what happened in the past. Release it and let God take care of you.

Don't allow people to dump their trashy thoughts on you! You are not a landfill where people are supposed to dump their garbage! Limit your time around people like that. Choose your mental diet carefully, for it will yield a harvest. Helen McInnes said, *"If we demand an honest statement of the ingredients of every package of food we buy, it seems odd that we should treat our minds more carelessly than we do our stomachs."*[4]

Stay away from things that have a negative effect upon you, such as certain reading materials, television and radio programs and certain places you may go. Listening to the wrong information only creates more obstacles in your mind for you to overcome. Censure what you watch, because the eyes are always gathering information to send to your mind.

Getting Rid Of
The Trash In Your Mind

If you find your mind has already been poisoned, there is still hope. I know people sometimes dump their trash on the doorstep of your mind before you can close the door! You can still rid your mind of those poisonous thoughts. Zig Ziglar said, *"Einstein pointed out that incorrect input requires eleven or more correct inputs to negate the erroneous information. This is another way of saying that it takes a number of 'right thinking' deposits to overcome those 'stinkin'-thinkin' deposits."*[10]

You can overcome negative thought patterns by taking a controlled and regular diet of correct material into your mind, and then letting the power of the Holy Spirit change your thinking. That is why you need to renew your mind by the daily *"washing of the Word"* (Ephesians 5:26). It is possible for you to be *"transformed by the renewing of your mind, that ye may prove what is that good, and acceptable, and perfect will of God"* (Romans 12:2).

Points To Ponder

1. The mind is able to remember everything that has happened in life, and assimilate thoughts and imaginations.

2. Two functions of the mind include recording new information and playing back what is recorded.

3. The mind gathers information through the conscience and the five physical senses.

4. Has your mind been poisoned? If so, choose a new diet from the scriptures. What scriptures do you need to use as correct input to dispel the incorrect input that has been put into your mind?

Chapter 4
TRANSFORMING THE MIND

And be not conformed to this world: but be ye transformed by the renewing of your mind, that ye may prove what is that good, and acceptable, and perfect will of God.
(Romans 12:2)

The society in which we live has everything as instant as we can make it. Fast food restaurants, convenience stores, instant cash machines, and multi-land highways are all affirmative of our "instant mentality." For some people, a major crisis occurs when they can't find the remote control for the television set so they can instantly flip to the channel they want to watch!

Some of the movies that Hollywood has put out give us a modern day image of the word "transform," by which a mere man can step into a telephone booth and instantly be transformed into a mighty superman wearing a body suit with a cape. But this is not the way change occurs in the human soul.

The word "transformed" in the Greek is the word *metamorphoo*. This is the same Greek word from which our English word "metamorphosis" is derived. It means to have a complete change of form, shape, or structure, and it indicates a process of change over a period of time.

This word is commonly used to describe the process whereby a caterpillar eventually changes into a beautiful butterfly. It takes time for this change to take place. It doesn't happen instantaneously, or even overnight.

This is what happens as you start the renewal process of daily reading the Word of God and letting the Holy Spirit do His work in you. When you become a Christian, your mind is like an ugly caterpillar, predominantly filled with the ugly thoughts of the world and the flesh. Your mind must go through the process of metamorphosis to become as a beautiful butterfly, expressing the beauty and purposes of God. You are then capable of going to the high places in life for which you were created. However, this takes time to happen.

Soulish things change through a process over a period of time, which is why you need to hear the same information over and over again. You need the continual *"...washing of the water by the Word"* (Ephesians 5:26) to cleanse your mind from harmful thoughts, ideas, imaginations, and memories. This brings out the value of daily devotions in the Word of God. You are cleansing your mind of the things of the world, and directing the thoughts of the Word of God into your mind. Renewing your mind with thoughts from the Word of God will lift you up into new realms of living you've never before experienced.

"PUTTING OFF" OLD THOUGHTS & "PUTTING ON" GOD'S THOUGHTS

See, I have this day set thee over the nations and over the kingdoms, to root out, and to pull down, and to destroy, and to throw down, to build, and to plant.
(Jeremiah 1:10)

In this verse, God reveals a process to Jeremiah. Both negative and positive events take place to complete the process of change so that you can move to higher realms of living. Notice the things that are mentioned: (1) to root out (2) to pull down (3) to destroy (3) to throw down (5) to plant, and (6) to build.

Many people play "dodge ball" with potentially negative situations to try to maintain peace of mind. They try to ignore the problem or will not admit to the negative conditions that may be present. But many times it is necessary to first root out, pull down, destroy and throw down things out of the soul before you can successfully plant and build the things you want there. *You cannot move up to new levels of life with old things hanging on you.* If you attempt to do so, these old things will undermine your progress, and when you least expect it (when the pressure is greatest, and the moment is most crucial) these old things will cause you to stumble and fall.

A prosperous soul is one in which negative ideas, thoughts, imaginations, and attitudes have been rooted out, pulled down, destroyed, and thrown down. Then new ideas and thoughts, which are in agreement with the Word of God and the level of life you want to live, are planted and built into the soul.

When a person remodels a kitchen, there is a tearing out phase that must take place before he can install the new fixtures. He must first take out all the old fixtures, and probably the old floor covering because it won't go with the new fixtures. Nothing positive seems to be happening in the initial "destruction" stage, unless one keeps in mind that he is simply doing this to make room for the new things desired in the kitchen.

By the same token, tearing out the old things is not enough either. There comes a time to install the new floor covering, cabinets and fixtures. When the kitchen remodeling project is finally finished, one will have gone through both the "tearing out" and the "building" stages.

If so be that ye have heard him, and have been taught by him, as the truth is Jesus: That ye PUT OFF concerning the former conversation the old man, which is corrupt according to the deceitful lusts; And be renewed in the spirit of your mind; And that ye PUT ON the new man, which after God is created in righteousness and true holiness.
(Ephesians 4:21-24)

29

But now ye also PUT OFF all these; anger, wrath, malice, blasphemy, filthy communication out of your mouth. Lie not one to another, seeing that ye have PUT OFF the old man with his deeds; And have PUT ON the new man, which is renewed in knowledge after the image of him that created him:
(Colossians 3:8-10)

Paul instructed believers to "put off" the old man and "put on" the new man. Both are necessary if you're going to get where God wants you to be. You do this by changing the attitudes of your mind. Embracing what God's Word tells you will cause change to take place in your mind.

Even some secular teachers and motivational speakers have picked up on this principle of letting go of something and taking hold of something new. One person calls it the "pain/pleasure" principle. Put off what is painful and restrictive and which keeps you from being what God wants you to be. Put on what is pleasing to God and His will for you.

It is not enough to identify and concentrate on stopping a particular habit or action. After you have identified the problem you must then concentrate on the answer. When a person concentrates only on what he wants to get rid of, he focuses so much on what he doesn't want that he ends up doing what he was trying to get rid of. The key is replacing what you don't want with what you want to start doing.

Harold Hill said in his book HOW TO FLIP YOUR FLAB FOREVER, *"Denial breeds compulsion."*[1] This explains why many people on a diet are not successful in losing weight. They are concentrating too much on what they can't have (food) or want to rid themselves of (their weight). Not only do they have to identify what they want to get rid of but they also must focus on what they want to obtain (better health, more energy, better appearance, more confidence, etc.).

Simply denying yourself of something is not enough. You must also concentrate on replacing what you're trying to get out of your life with what you want to put into your life.

TRANSFORMED IN THE GLORY OF GOD

But we all, with open face beholding as in a glass the glory of the Lord, are changed into the same image from glory to glory, even as by the Spirit of the Lord.
(2 Corinthians 3:18)

In this verse the word "changed" is the same Greek word "metamorphosis" translated "transformed" in **Romans 12:2**. This verse reveals that the Holy Spirit also has a major role in the transformation of your mind. It is not only about putting off old thoughts and putting on the thoughts found in the Word of God. There are times when the Holy Spirit manifests Himself in the midst of His people, and in that atmosphere of glory, changes which could not be accomplished any other way can take place in the lives of those who yield to His work.

You will not become the person God wants you to be unless you are willing to get into a place where the glory of God is being manifested and let Him have His way. In the atmosphere of God's glory, Satan cannot withstand you and your mind will not resist God's thoughts as much. Somehow, in the glory of God, your little human thoughts don't matter as much anymore and you come to the place where you want to think the thoughts of God.

There is a price to pay for getting into the glory of God. Do what you must in order to get into a place where God's glory is being manifested. Mark Hankins said, *"Some changes must happen before the glory can come, but the glory must also come before some changes can be made."*[2] In other words, you must make some preparation for the glory of God to manifest, but the glory of God will cause the changes you need in your life to come about.

You must put off old thoughts and put on new thoughts from the Word of God. You must also receive change in your thought life by getting into the place where God's glory is being manifested, and submitting to the work of the Holy Spirit.

TRANSFORMATION OF THE MIND IS ONGOING

Who delivered us from so great a death, and doth deliver: in whom we trust that he will yet deliver us;
(2 Corinthians 1:10)

Mark Hankins said, *"Your mind does not stay renewed anymore than your hair stays combed."*[3] You must realize that the process of changing the soul is ongoing. It is continuous, no matter how far you've come. This is how the soul functions. Notice in 2 Corinthians 1:10 that three different phases are mentioned: delivered (past tense), being delivered (present tense), and will be delivered (future tense). When you were born again you were delivered (past tense) in your spirit. God is also daily delivering (present tense) your soul as it is renewed by the Word of God. It is an ongoing process that is presently happening. And, like Paul, you are to trust that God will yet deliver (future tense) your bodies.

This explains why a person can have a spiritual experience on Sunday and act carnal on Monday. The process of changing the soul is not yet complete. Some people receive from God one day and act very immature the next day because their minds are not fully transformed.

In fact, even those who are committed to Christ, and are dedicated to the work of Christ may experience feelings that vary, and conflicting thoughts may try to get in their minds. God doesn't intend for you to live your life guided by your feelings, but it is not abnormal to have feelings that vary. You must learn to govern your thoughts and feelings with the Word of God if you are going to maintain the victory God wants you to have.

Has anyone ever done something to you that brought out the "unrenewed" part of your mind? Perhaps someone made a snide remark, or did something stupid while driving in front of you, or your extra efforts to complete the project you had been working on weren't valued. Different things cause people to react in a carnal way.

We know we're not to yield to that part of our soul. Thank God for the Holy Spirit who dwells in your born again spirit on the inside of you; He will remind you to think and walk according to the Word of God while you are in the process of obtaining a renewed mind. The good news is that while you are renewing your mind, God will strengthen you, keep you, and sustain you by the Holy Spirit.

Just remember that what God has started, He will also finish. God does not give up on you, so don't give up on yourself!

Study the following scriptures until you are confident that God will keep working in you until your mind is renewed with His Word, and you are moving up into new realms of life.

The Lord will perfect that which concerneth me: thy mercy, O Lord, endureth for ever: forsake not the works of thine own hands.
(Psalms 138:8)

Being confident of this very thing, that he which hath begun a good work in you will perform it until the day of Jesus Christ:
(Philippians 1:6)

Looking unto Jesus the author and finisher of our faith ...
(Hebrews 12:2)

POINTS TO PONDER

1. SOULISH THINGS CHANGE THROUGH A PROCESS, AND IT TAKES TIME.

2. BOTH NEGATIVE AND POSITIVE EVENTS TAKE PLACE TO COMPLETE THE PROCESS OF CHANGE.

3. THE PROCESS OF CHANGING THE SOUL IS ONGOING. IT IS CONTINUOUS, NO MATTER HOW FAR YOU'VE COME.

4. WHAT ARE SOME OLD THOUGHTS YOU NEED TO PUT OFF? WHAT ARE SOME NEW THOUGHTS YOU NEED TO BRING INTO YOUR MIND?

Chapter 5

CONTROLLING
YOUR THOUGHTS

*Don't let the world around you squeeze you into its own
mold, but let God remake you so that your whole attitude
is changed ... Thus you will prove in practice that the will
of God is good, acceptable to him, and perfect.*
(Romans 12:2, Phillips)

I can still remember some of the goals I had when I was a
child. They were noble goals, as most children's aspirations are.
When I was in the eighth grade, I set some very specific goals,
financially, morally, and socially; but in a few short years I had
strayed far from these goals. Why did that happen? Primarily it
was because I didn't know the truths presented in this chapter.

There are things in the world around you that will influence
your thinking if you allow it. If you are aware of these
"influencers" you can safeguard your soul from them, and you
can develop a prosperous soul. Actually, when you understand
the principles these "influencers" use, you can use them for
your good.

These "influencers" can limit what you will be, what you do,
and where you live. They can also release you into the full
potential of what you can be and how far you move up in life.
You must learn to work these influences to your benefit if you
want to break into new realms of living and achievement. You
cannot afford to ignore them or take them lightly. At first glance
they may seem superficial, but they have the ability to shape the
very core of your soul.

Almost all the things that influence your soul in this world can be put into three categories. They consist of (1) your diet (2) your associates, and (3) your environment. As you learn how to control the influence of each of these areas, you will grow in your Christian walk and you will be more successful in doing what God wants you to do. You will be able to move forward into the realms of life God has promised to you.

These three categories influence your soul through your five physical senses. Remember that your mind gathers information about the world in which you live through the five physical senses. Your five physical senses gather most of their information from these three categories, so you can readily see why these three categories are very important. Let's take a close look at each of these "influencers" to understand the impact they have upon your thinking.

What Kind Of Diet Are You On?

The greatest influence upon your soul is your spiritual and mental diet. You cannot rise higher than the level of the material that is put in you. *"You will be the same five years from now except for two things (1) the books you read (2) the people you hang around with."*[1] (Charles "Tremendous" Jones).

Control your spiritual and mental intake by limiting what you watch and listen to on television and radio. The best that you can do with television and radio is select the station or channel. But you cannot choose the programming on these channels. Don't put your progress in life at the mercy of someone on television or radio, especially if you don't know his beliefs or values.

Always ask yourself questions like (1) "Does this have the same beliefs and values I have?" (2) "Is this promoting the goals and performance level I want to achieve?" or (3) "Will this help me move up to where God wants me to be in life?" Use things like books, audio cassette tapes, or video tapes that you can control.

Listen to the sermons and teachings of men and women of God who have achieved great things. Let yourself be inspired as you read their biographies. This will lift you to a new level of thinking, vision, and living. It will also help you believe that it is possible to achieve your God-given dream.

1 Corinthians 14:10 tells us, *"There are, it may be, so many kinds of voices in the world, and none of them is without signification."* Many things vie for your attention and all of them seem to have something to say. But are they in agreement with the Word of God, and do they reflect where you know God wants you to be?

There are many good preachers and teachers today on Christian television and radio, but have you noticed they are saying many different things? If you spend all your time watching these ministers and receive everything they say, you will become confused. Too many different voices saying too many different things will cause you to feel as if you're being pulled in ten different directions at once.

Focus what you read, hear, and see in the areas that you want to grow in or move toward. This will accelerate the growth of your soul, and eliminate confusion from your mind.

A steady diet of the Word of God causes the Word to gain prominence in your thinking, and you will be able to discern whether or not to accept what someone is saying to you.

YOUR FRIENDS & ASSOCIATES

Enter not into the path of the wicked, and go not in the way of evil men. Avoid it, pass not by it, turn from it, and pass away. For they sleep not, except they have done mischief; and their sleep is taken away, unless they cause some to fall.

(Proverbs 4:14-16)

People usually decide who their friends are by whomever is friendly to them. Most people do not ask or pay any attention to the beliefs and values of the people they have for friends.

All relationships are one of four kinds – those who add, multiply, subtract, or divide. Identify each relationship honestly. Mike Murdock said, *"Friendships are based upon mutual interests or problems. Be sure you know the difference."*[2] He added, *"Those who do not increase you, inevitably will decrease you."*[3]

Bob Harrison stated, *"Birds of a feather flock together. But that's not the end of the story. The end of the story is that they all fly to the same place!"* Another person said, *"Thirty percent of your associates should be those who can lift you up to their level."* Your close associates and those you continually hang around with will have great influence on the outcome of your life.

You should carefully cultivate both an inner circle of friends and an outer circle of acquaintances. Your inner circle of friends should consist of those who hold the same beliefs and values that you do. They should be those who are able to help each other climb higher in life, support each other, believe in one another, and are loyal to one another.

Your outer circle of friends will be those who are friendly toward you, but they do not necessarily hold the same values and beliefs that you do. In other words, if you followed them, you would not get where you want to go.

Jesus illustrated this in His earthly ministry. There were seventy people who were acquainted with Jesus well enough to be used in ministry, but they weren't named in scripture. Jesus also had twelve disciples, or followers, who were associated with Him closely enough that they were a part of His personal ministry team, and they were mentioned by name in scripture.

However, of the twelve disciples, Jesus chose only three disciples, Peter, James, and John, with whom He shared His special moments. This included the raising of Jairus' daughter **(Mark 5:37)**, the transfiguration **(Mark 9:2)**, and the Garden of Gethsemane **(Mark 14:32-33)**. Even beyond that, Jesus entrusted His mother to only one of his disciples: John.

Jesus loved everybody. He helped everyone who would receive it. Jesus was moved with compassion for the multitudes, but He never became a friend with the multitudes. He was not a friend with everyone. His friends consisted of those who had the same values and beliefs that He did.

Jesus was lifted up and strengthened to finish what He came into the earth to do because He spent time with His Father. The Father lifted Jesus up above the limitations of other peoples' thinking until Jesus was able to do, say, and act as His Father would. Jesus showed us the importance of spending time with the right people so we will arrive at the right place. Because Jesus spent quality time with the Father, He was seated at the right hand of God the Father for eternity!

What do you do when a close friend of yours no longer exhibits the same beliefs and values that you have? Do you end the relationship, or should you overlook it? **Romans 12:18** says, *"If it be possible, as much as lieth in you, live peaceably with all men."* You should never burn bridges if you can avoid it. Do not end the relationship, but do not just overlook it either.

Gradually move that person from your inner circle of associates to your outer circle of acquaintances. This means you limit the time you spend with him, and you are careful how you receive what he has to say. The reason you don't want to end the relationship is because you want to leave the door open so you can help him, or lift him up to your level, should the opportunity arise.

As you progress in the plan God has for your life, your close associates may change. This is a normal process of growth. One reason for this is because they may not be headed in the same direction God is taking you. Also, they may not be growing at the pace you are growing and you have to leave them behind in order to reach the place God wants you to be.

You cannot take everybody with you on the path God has called you to go. Not all your friends are called to go that way. Concentrate on those who are going the same way you are going. Love everybody, but limit your friends to those who have the same values and beliefs that you do.

THE ENVIRONMENT YOU LIVE IN

Do not conform any longer to the pattern of this world, but be transformed by the renewing of your mind. Then you will be able to test and approve what God's will is – his good, pleasing and perfect will. (Romans 12:2, NIV)

Your environment includes many things, such as your surroundings and your circumstances. It also includes where your experiences in life take place.

The places that people continually go and the environment they live in have great influence upon their thinking. Most people habitually go to the same places. They have a circle of places that is "their world." Often this influences their decision of what they think is acceptable or what they can afford.

The world spends all their efforts on food, clothing, and shelter. This is their way of thinking; survival is the name of the game. Be careful that in the midst of your daily life, you don't let the world's way of living influence your thinking.

You are to seek God who freely provides all things to you. Keep God first in your life; this allows Him to be your provider, and your limitations won't be determined by what your job pays you. You will then be a greater blessing in life.

Another way our environment influences us is through our religious environments. Some churches teach that God does not care about your circumstances or conditions. Others teach that God will only supply your needs, but not your wants. Therefore, many people end up with a cheap picture of God because they have substituted the teachings of men for the Word of God. This is the reason many people are barely getting by. *They are operating in the perimeters formed by man's words instead of in the freedom of the promises of God's Word.*

If you can control the input from these three areas in your life you can greatly control your thought life, and ultimately control your output in life.

Points To Ponder

1. Name three areas that are great "influencers" in your thought life.

2. What mental and spiritual diet should you be on?

3. Do you have friends you need to move to the outer circle? Are they helping or hindering you?

4. Has your environment been hindering your thinking? What can you change in your environment to create a positive influence in your thought life?

Chapter 6

EXAMINING YOUR WILL

Another part of the human soul is the will. The next two chapters deal with defining the will and how to conform the human will to God's will. When your will is consecrated and conformed to God's will, you can make great strides in following God and moving up into new realms of God's promises.

Remember what Dr. Jerry Savelle said: *"A prosperous soul is one in which the mind is renewed, the will conformed, the emotions controlled, and the thinking faculties selective of that which it thinks."*[1]

DEFINING THE HUMAN WILL

The human will can be defined as man's control over impulse. Sometimes a person is referred to as "having a strong will" or having the ability to control his impulses. The word "will" comes from the Greek word *thelema* which means *determination, choice, purpose, decree, desire, pleasure, and inclination.*

Man's will is designed to be in submission, either to God's will or to Satan's will. For example, when a person is in rebellion to God, he has submitted his will to Satan's will. Man's will cannot be exercised independently from God or Satan's will. It will always operate under the influence of either one or the other.

A few years ago Frank Sinatra sang a song that said, "I Did It My Way," but the truth is that nobody does it their own way. Either God's will or Satan's will is influencing the human will.

When someone thinks he did it his own way he is believing a lie. Invisible, spiritual forces are influencing people, often without those people being conscious of their presence.

GOD HAS A WILL

Thou art worthy, O Lord, to receive glory and honour and power: for thou hast created all things, and for thy pleasure they are and were created.
(Revelation 4:11)

The word "pleasure" in **Revelation 4:11** comes from the same Greek word that is also translated "will." So we see that God's will and God's pleasure are connected and operate in agreement. All things were originally created to be pleasing to God and in agreement with God's will. It pleased God to exercise His will to create man; therefore man is a product of both God's will and His pleasure.

Which were born, not of blood, nor the will of the flesh, not the will of man, but of God.
(John1:13)

Here we see that Jesus was born, not by man's will, but by the will of God. **John 6:38** tells us He lived and ministered by the will of God. *"For I came down from heaven, not to do mine own will, but the will of him that sent me."* Also Jesus, by the will of God, gave Himself for our sins. *"Who gave himself for our sins, that he might deliver us from this present evil world, according to the will of God and our Father."* (Galatians 1:4)

The Word of God contains the will of God. They cannot be separated. God is not a man that He should lie. God's will has been written in His Word. Just as Jesus came in the flesh to reveal the will of the Father, so the written Word also reveals the will of God to us.

SATAN ALSO HAS A WILL

How art thou fallen from heaven, O Lucifer, son of the morning! how art thou cut down to the ground, which didst weaken the nations!

For thou hast said in thine heart, I will ascend into heaven, I will exalt my throne above the stars of God: I will sit also upon the mount of the congregation, in the sides of the north.

I will ascend above the heights of the clouds; I will be like the most High.

(Isaiah 14:12-14)

In **Isaiah 14:12-14** we read what I call the five "I wills" of Satan. Here Satan exercised his will against God's will. A person exercising his will against God's will is committing iniquity or sin; this is why Satan was cast out of heaven.

EXAMPLES OF THE HUMAN WILL

And the Lord said, Behold, the people is one, and they have all one language; and this they begin to do; and now nothing will be restrained from them, which they have imagined to do.

(Genesis 11:6)

The Hebrew word used for "imagination" includes the idea of the human will. Imaginations and the human will are connected and usually operate in agreement. By exercising their will, these people began to set the limits to their own lives.

...we all had our conversation in times past in the lusts of our flesh, fulfilling the desires of the flesh and of the mind; and were by nature the children of wrath...

(Ephesians 2:3)

Ephesians 2:3 describes man while he was still a sinner - *"...the children of wrath"* who had a lifestyle *"in the lusts of* *their flesh.*" Throughout the Word of God the descriptions of man's condition reflects either God's character and attributes, or Satan's character. This reveals that man's will cannot operate independently from either Godly or Satanic influence.

While a sinner, man did what he thought he wanted to do. However, if a person does not exercise their will in agreement with God's will, they are simply conforming to Satan's desires.

If ye be willing and obedient, ye shall eat the good of the land:
(Isaiah 1:19)

Notice that being both willing and obedient to do what God tells you to do are necessary to you can enjoy the good things God has promised to you.

Have you ever met someone who was obedient but grumbled while obeying? Even though he was doing what he was told, he still had a rebellious attitude. However, the blessing of God comes when we conform our will to what He said and then obey Him.

And Simon answering said unto him, Master, we have toiled all the night, and have taken nothing; nevertheless at thy word I will let down the net.
(Luke 5:5)

Peter conformed his will to do what Jesus said, and reaped great benefits because of it. Often the supply we need comes when we conform our will to God's Word and then obey Him.

IDENTIFYING STRONG SOULISH DESIRES

Sometimes people have a difficult time identifying the will of God because they have nurtured strong, soulish desires for a long time. Many Christians do not separate strong, soulish desires they have cultivated for years (especially while growing up) from the will of God. As a result they get confused because they thought they heard the voice of God, and it didn't happen the way they thought God said it would.

Soulish desires that are not identified and dealt with can interfere with doing the will of God. Soulish desires have a strong voice, so you must learn to separate this voice from God's will if you want to follow God and have what He has said you can have.

If you exercise your will according to these soulish desires and not according to the will of God, your soul may experience turmoil and agony. After Eve disobeyed God, He told her she would experience sorrow in her soul.

Unto the woman he said, I will greatly multiply thy sorrow and thy conception; in sorrow thou shalt bring forth children; and thy desire shall be to thy husband, and he shall rule over thee.

(Genesis 3:16)

Here is an excerpt from SPIRITUAL HUNGER by John G. Lake that reveals the power of soulish desires and the human will:

"When I was a lad, I accompanied my father on a visit to the office of John A. McCall, the great insurance man. We were taken to McCall's office in his private elevator. It was the first time I had ever been in a great office building and ridden in an elevator, and I held my breath until the thing stopped. Then we stepped into his office, the most beautiful office I ever had beheld. The rugs were so thick I was afraid I would go through the floor when I stepped on them. His desk was a marvel, pure mahogany, and on top of his desk, inlaid in mother-of-pearl, was his name, written in script. It was so magnificent that in by boyish soul I said, "I am going to have an office just like this, and a desk like that with my name on it when I am a man."

I did not know until I was in my thirtieth year how strong that was in my nature. It almost seemed to be forgotten. I was invited to Chicago to join an association of men who were establishing a life insurance company. They said, "Lake, we want you to be manager of this association." We discussed the matter for three weeks until they came to my terms, and finally the president said, "Step into this office. I want to show you something. We have a surprise for you." I stepped into an office that was the exact duplicate of John A. McCall's office, and there in the center was a desk of pure mahogany. Instead of the name of John A. McCall, it was John G. Lake inscribed in mother-of-pearl. I had never spoken of that soul-desire to a person in the world. There is something in the call of a soul that is creative. It brings things to pass."[2]

Exercising the power of the human will can cause things to come to pass. However, unless your willpower is conformed to God's will you may be opening the door to things that God doesn't want for you. If you go far enough in this area you might start operating in witchcraft as you force your will upon other people against their wishes, and exercise your will against God's will.

Since you can exercise your will against God's will, it is important that you conform your will to God's will.

POINTS TO PONDER

1. MAN HAS A WILL DESIGNED TO BE IN SUBMISSION, EITHER TO GOD'S WILL OR SATAN'S WILL.

2. IT IS NECESSARY TO BE BOTH WILLING AND OBEDIENT TO WHAT GOD TELLS YOU TO DO SO YOU CAN ENJOY THE GOOD THINGS GOD HAS PROMISED TO YOU.

3. SOULISH DESIRES THAT ARE NOT IDENTIFIED AND DEALT WITH CAN INTERFERE WITH DOING THE WILL OF GOD.

Chapter 6
CONFORMING YOUR WILL

And he went a little farther, and fell on his face, and prayed, saying, O my Father, if it be possible, let this cup pass from me: nevertheless not as I will, but as thou wilt... He went away again the second time, and prayed, saying, O my Father, if this cup may not pass away from me, except I drink it, thy will be done.
(Matthew 26:39,42)

CONFORMING TO THE WILL OF GOD

Many Christians admit that they seemingly have no will power to conform to God's will. How does a person conform his will completely to God's will? How do you get to the place where you are able to pray the prayer that Jesus prayed in the Garden of Gethsemane and mean it with all of your heart?

Conforming your will is a process, and must be done daily. It must be done as long as a person is serving God. The process of conforming your will can be broken down into the following four principles.

First of all, you must know God's will. You cannot act on something you don't know. Reading the Word of God will reveal God's will to you, and cause right thoughts to be put in your mind. Based upon the information received in your mind, your will either submits to or rebels against an issue. This forms the basis for conforming your will to fulfill God's will and desires. Pastor Billy Joe Daugherty said, *"When we assume that happiness and problem-free living are the goals we are after, we will never fulfill the will of God."*[1]

Teach me to do thy will; for thou art my God; thy spirit is
good; lead me into the land of uprightness.
(Psalms 143:10)

David said once he knew what the will of God was, he would
do it. The Holy Spirit taught him the will of God and led him into
the place of being right with God.

Secondly, you must understand your will and the forces
behind it. Peter J. Daniels states in his book, HOW TO REACH
YOUR LIFE GOALS, *"As the word itself suggests, willpower is*
putting power into the will from the desires created by interior
motives. Therefore, a strong, chain effect is exhibited rather
than a single decision of the will."[2]

What are your motives? Your motives reveal your desires,
which in turn fuel your will. Where do motives come from?
They are based upon the information and experiences that have
entered the mind. You can ensure right motives in every
situation if you have the Word of God as your primary desire.

This is why it is important to meditate upon the Word of God.
David said, *"Let the words of my mouth, and the meditation*
of my heart, be acceptable in thy sight, O Lord, my strength,
and my redeemer." (Psalms 19:14).

Thirdly, you must consecrate your will to God's will until
His will becomes yours. Then the will of God can come clearly
to the forefront of your thoughts in any given situation. This
takes time in prayer, reflection, and meditation upon God's
Word. You must be willing to lay down personal ambitions,
dreams, and desires.

To consecrate means to set apart. You must consecrate and
set yourself apart to the will of God daily. As you do so you will
be able to commit more and more to the will of God. Finally, you

get to the place where you can commit to and fulfill the will of God for your life.

Epaphras, who is one of you, a servant of Christ, saluteth you, always labouring fervently for you in prayers, that ye may stand perfect and complete in all the will of God.
(Colossians 4:12)

You'll never come to the place of great consecration without times of prayer. Epaphras labored fervently in prayer so that the Colossians would conform to the will of God until they were perfect and experienced the will of God completely.

In times of consecration, you must come to the revelation that without Christ you can do nothing (John 15:5). Along with this revelation you must also realize the truth of Philippians 4:13, *"I can do all things through Christ which strengtheneth me."* True consecration is entering the place where you desire to do nothing without Him, and do all things in Him.

Fourthly, you must commit your will to the will of God. Commitment is an act of trust, and therefore a person does not reach the place of commitment easily. You must grow into it. Being committed to the will of God is as important as knowing the will of God. Your commitment to the will of God determines the value of knowing it in the first place.

Being committed to the will of God means reaching a place of commitment to the Word of God. You cannot separate the will of God from the Word of God because they are one and the same. The way you relate to the Word of God is the way you will respond to the will of God.

I met a man in a restaurant one time and began to talk to him about Christianity. I found out that he didn't go to church and was living with his girlfriend. Then he told me that God spoke to him at one time to be an evangelist. I guess he thought that would impress me, but instead he was shocked when I asked him, "What are you doing about it?" This man knew the will of God for his life but it was of no value to him because he had made no commitment to it.

THE EXAMPLE OF THE THREE HEBREW MEN

Shadrach, Meshach, and Abednego, answered and said to the king, O Nebuchadnezzar, we are not careful to answer thee in this matter.

If it be so, our God whom we serve is able to deliver us from the burning fiery furnace, and he will deliver us out of thine hand, O king.

But if not, be it known unto thee, O king, that we will not serve thy gods, nor worship the golden image which thou hast set up.

(Daniel 3:16-18)

The three Hebrew men who refused to bow to the image of Nebuchadnezzar were committed to the will of God, whether that meant being delivered, or being burned in the fire.

THE EXAMPLE OF JESUS

Jesus recognized the Old Testament scriptures as the will of God for Him. A study of Jewish history reveals that Jewish boys were required to spend many hours learning the scriptures. Jesus probably spent many hours studying the Old Testament scriptures as a boy growing up. When He was tempted in the wilderness by the devil, He responded in every case, *"It is written..."* (Matthew 4:4,7,10). Jesus referred to the scripture as the basis for His conduct, His direction, His defense, and His destiny.

Jesus withdrew himself from other people on a regular basis to pray (**Matthew 26:36, Mark 6:46, 14:32, Luke 6:12, 9:28**). He sought the instruction and will of the Father in prayer. During these times of prayer Jesus both received knowledge of specific issues concerning the will of God and consecrated himself to the will of God.

Jesus also committed himself to the will of the Father. In **John 4:34** He said, *"My meat is to do the will of him that sent me, and to finish his work."* The value of Jesus knowing the will of God and coming to the earth was determined by His consecration and commitment to the plan and will of God which brought him there. He did this by committing to what His Father said.

For I have not spoken of myself; but the Father which sent me, he gave me a commandment, what I should say, and what I should speak.
And I know that his commandment is life everlasting: whatsoever I speak therefore, even as the Father said unto me, so I speak.
(John 12:49-50)

Then said Jesus unto them, When ye have lifted up the Son of man, then shall ye know that I am he, and that I do nothing of myself; but as my Father hath taught me, I speak these things.
(John 8:28)

Jesus indicated that if a person will commit to the Word of God, it will enable him to do what the Word of God tells him. Make a commitment to the Word of God daily. It is impossible to conform to God's will without first making a commitment to His Word.

Jesus lived thirty-three years upon the earth, and during that time He grew and developed to the place where He could commit himself to finish the work of redemption by enduring the cross, death, and the grave. It took thirty-three years of growth and development so that Jesus could commit to the prayer He prayed in the Garden of Gethsemane.

...Father, if thou be willing, remove this cup from me: nevertheless not my will, but thine, be done.

(Luke 22:42)

Jesus proved it is possible for you to consecrate and commit your life to God's Word until you are able to do what God wants you to do. By following Jesus' example it is possible for you to say as He did in **John 17:4**, *"I have glorified thee on the earth: I have finished the work which thou gavest me to do."*

POINTS TO PONDER

1. CONFORMING YOUR WILL INVOLVES (1) KNOWING GOD'S WILL (2) KNOWING YOUR OWN WILL AND THE FORCES BEHIND IT (3) CONSECRATING YOUR WILL TO GOD'S WILL (4) COMMITTING TO GOD'S WILL.

2. THE VALUE OF KNOWING THE WILL OF GOD IS DETERMINED BY YOUR COMMITMENT TO IT.

3. YOU MUST DAILY CONSECRATE AND SET YOURSELF APART TO THE WILL OF GOD.

4. BEING COMMITTED TO THE WILL OF GOD MEANS REACHING A PLACE OF COMMITMENT TO THE WORD OF GOD.

Chapter 8

DEALING WITH
YOUR EMOTIONS

D r. Jerry Savelle said, *"A prosperous soul is one in which the mind is renewed, the will conformed, the emotions controlled, and the thinking faculties selective of that which it thinks."*[1] In this chapter we will examine another part of the soul – the human emotions. Let's see what the Word of God has to say about the emotions, because the Word of God is really the only solid foundation for studying and ministering to the emotions.

The human emotions have been a rather controversial subject in the Body of Christ. Some advocate that everything in your past contributes to, or determines, your present emotional state. Others deny their emotions the right to function, and do not allow them to be expressed at all.

DEFINING THE HUMAN EMOTIONS

The word "emotions" comes from the Latin word *emotus* meaning *"to move out."* People are more easily moved in their emotions than in almost any other area of their beings. Emotions include the capacity for feelings and affections such as love, hate, joy, and fear. Emotions also have to do with your consciousness, which is shown by your feelings and affections.

The word "emotions" is not found in the King James Version of the Bible. However, the Greek language shows that the word "affections" is akin to the emotions.

THE INFLUENCE OF THE EMOTIONS

Proverbs 4:23, (TLB) reveals the importance of the emotions in a human being: *"Above all else, guard your affections, for they influence everything else in your life."* Dale Carnegie said, *"When dealing with people, let us remember that we are not dealing with creatures of logic. We are dealing with creatures of emotion."*[2]

The Word of God instructs Christians where to set their affections in **Colossians 3:1-2,** *"If ye then be risen with Christ, seek those things which are above, where Christ sitteth on the right hand of God. Set your affection on things above, not on things on the earth."* Mark Hankins said, *"Your affections will determine your direction."*[3] People usually go in the direction of their affections and passions. Someone sent me a card one time that said, *"There are many things in life that will catch your eye, but only a few will catch your heart... pursue those."*[4]

Focus your affections and emotions in the areas that you want to excel in. You cannot achieve great things while being affectionate of little things. The greatest people in history have learned to control and direct their affections and emotions in the direction that they wanted to go.

SCRIPTURAL EXAMPLES OF HUMAN EMOTIONS & AFFECTIONS

God gave some people with perverted relationships over to vile *affections* and lusts **(Romans 1:26; Colossians 3:5)**. Some people's involvement in certain things cause them to be without *natural affections* and the ability to cherish *affectionately*, and they become hard-hearted **(Romans 1:31; Titus 3:3)**.

Paul *affectionately desired and longed for* the Thessalonian church **(1 Thessalonians 2:8)**. Titus had an inward affection (fig. tender mercy, sympathy, and pity) toward the Corinthian church **(2 Corinthians 7:13-15)**.

Believers are to crucify the flesh with its affections, emotions, and influences. Crucifixion involves something undergone with hardship or pain, indicating that a death is necessary **(Galatians 5:24)**. Believers are to set their affections, sentiments, and opinions on things above **(Colossians 3:2)**.

EXAMINING YOUR EMOTIONS

For the word of God is quick, and powerful, and sharper than any twoedged sword, piercing even to the dividing asunder of soul and spirit, and of the joints and marrow, and is a discerner of the thoughts and intents of the heart.
(Hebrews 4:12)

The Word of God is alive and powerful, and has the ability to penetrate and do a work in your soul and spirit. Just as a sword is able to penetrate the physical body, the Word of God, under the direction of the Holy Spirit, is powerful and able to go into your soul and spirit and accomplish the will of God.

Emotions are often buried in the "subconscious" mind, or the human spirit. Emotions can be ministered to by the Word of God in controlled situations with the right atmosphere, and when confronted with the help of the Holy Spirit. At times the Holy Spirit will bring to your conscious mind certain emotions and feelings that are hindering your Christian development. As this happens, you can identify them and deal with them effectively according to the Word of God.

That is why you need to take "Word baths" according to **Ephesians 5:26** on a regular and continual basis. Reading the Word of God, believing it, and then speaking the Word to yourself will create an atmosphere that allows the Holy Spirit to reveal your emotions and desires to you.

When silver is purified, the dross which comes to the surface can be removed. It may have to be done several times, but the end result of this refining process is pure silver. Just as silver is purified through the refining process, your soul can also be purified through the fire of the Holy Spirit as He applies the Word of God. The "impurities" of your soul, such as hurts, wounds, and bruises, can be removed from the emotional arena when they come to the surface of your conscious mind by the work of the Holy Spirit.

Charles Allen said, *"The human mind is like the human body. It can be wounded. Sorrow is a wound. It cuts deeply, but sorrow is a clean wound, and will heal unless something gets into the wound, such as bitterness, self-pity, or resentment... the most expensive thing you can do is hold a wrong spirit in your heart against another. The price you pay is the loss, the eternal loss, of your own soul."*[5] You need to keep your heart and soul clean if you want your entire being to be healthy.

Acknowledge the problem, affirm God's ability to help, and ask for God's help. These steps are necessary in dealing with your emotions. This is how you received salvation, and the principles can be used in dealing with your emotions.

First of all, acknowledge the existence of the emotional hurts, wounds, and bruises. This is necessary to both yourself and to God. Also, acknowledge your own inability to deal with those hurts, wounds, and bruises to God.

Secondly, affirm God's ability to take care of those hurts, wounds, and bruises by quoting scriptures that relate to your situation.

Thirdly, ask God to deal with your hurts, wounds, and bruises with His forgiveness and enable you to forgive by the power of the Holy Spirit. Learn to rely upon God's ability to do what you cannot do in your soul; however, He needs your permission to work there.

Galatians 5:24 tells you to crucify the affections and emotions of the flesh, revealing that a death to your fleshly emotions and desires is necessary. This does not happen instantaneously; rather it is a process over a period of time. In **1 Corinthians 15:31** Paul said, *"...I die daily."*

One day I was talking with a hospital chaplain about people who find out there is no hope for them to recover and that death is inevitable. He told me there are five basic stages such people go through emotionally. The five basic stages are (1) denial (2) anger (3) bargaining (4) depression (5) acceptance. (Acceptance does not mean they have accepted the facts presented to them; rather it means being able to live and function in spite of the reports or events that have taken place.)

This process applies not only to those who are dying but also to anyone who has suffered abuse or loss of any kind. This helps you understand the process you are going through emotionally, helps you measure your progress, and shows why you are acting in a certain way. No matter where you are in the process of dealing with emotional problems, the Word of God can help you as you believe it and speak it. Remember, **Ephesians 5:26** states that you are to be, *"sanctified and cleansed by the washing of the water of the Word."*

Several years ago I met a man named John who had experienced severe emotional damage as a child. John's story of how he recovered from extreme emotional damage will give you hope in dealing with your emotional problems.

John grew up in a very authoritarian home and church setting. He was abused physically, sexually, nutritionally, and emotionally. John tried hard to please his father, but found it was impossible to do so. His parent's marriage was constantly in strife and ended when his father died of cancer in John's young adult life.

Fear from what John had seen his parents go through in their marriage kept him from getting married. He tried to get free of the authoritarian church he grew up in but could not break its legalistic hold. He became involved in drugs and occult activity. When John was forty years old he became born again and left the church he had grown up in, only to find himself in another church worse than the one he had been in before.

Finally, after much teaching, encouragement, and support, John was set free by the power of the Word of God and the work of the Holy Spirit. Now he is attending a church where he can grow spiritually. He is free in his mind and can think the thoughts of God's Word, control his emotions, and is conforming his will to God's will. He has worked his way throughout the process to emotional wholeness, and is now healed from those emotional wounds suffered as a child. However, it was a process of getting his soul and emotions healed, and building the thoughts of God's Word into his soul.

POINTS TO PONDER

1. THE WORD OF GOD IS ALIVE, POWERFUL, AND HAS THE ABILITY TO PENETRATE AND DO A WORK IN YOUR SOUL AND SPIRIT.

2. "ABOVE ALL ELSE, GUARD YOUR AFFECTIONS, FOR THEY INFLUENCE EVERYTHING ELSE IN YOUR LIFE."

3. ACKNOWLEDGE THE PROBLEM, AFFIRM GOD'S ABILITY TO HELP, AND ASK FOR GOD'S HELP. THESE STEPS ARE NECESSARY IN DEALING WITH EMOTIONS.

4. THE FIVE BASIC STAGES TO EMOTIONAL WHOLENESS ARE (1) DENIAL (2) ANGER (3) BARGAINING (4) DEPRESSION (5) ACCEPTANCE.

Chapter 9

CONTROLLING YOUR EMOTIONS

MINISTERING TO YOUR SOUL & EMOTIONS

When I was a young minister I could not preach without crying. Even though I studied the Word, I was an emotional person. I began to seek the Lord for an answer. How could I control my emotions?

One day as I was studying **Isaiah 53:5**, I saw that Christ had provided for my whole being: spirit, soul, and body at Calvary. *"But He was wounded for our transgressions, He was bruised for our iniquities"* applied to my spirit, *"the chastisement of our peace was upon His"* applied to my soul, and *"by His stripes we are healed"* applied to my physical body.

God began to show me the importance of applying the Word of God to this area of my soul. I began to believe and speak the Word of God over my soul. I applied my faith in God's Word toward my soul just like any other area in which I had a need. As I began to believe and speak the Word of God, it created an arena wherein my soul could act, and it set boundaries for the actions of my soul.

As I applied the Word of God, it undergirded the weaknesses and flaws in my soul. I began to experience strength I had not had before, and I was able to resist the impulses and emotional cravings in my soul which were not in line with the Word of God.

One of the greatest blessings I have experienced in the area of my soul is being set free from low self-esteem. As I began to read and study **Ephesians 1:3-13**, I began to see how God looked at me, what He had already done for me at Calvary, and who I was in Christ as a believer. When I saw in **Ephesians 1:6** that God had already accepted me, I realized that other peoples' acceptance or non-acceptance of me was not to dictate my value and self-worth.

The Word of God is the one thing that will consistently minister to your emotions. There is no substitute for the Word of God in ministering to your soul. As you read the Word, let it be a healing balm to your soul, like water to a parched body. There may be other spiritual applications you need that will help your emotions, along with applying the Word of God. However, you should always apply the Word of God even if there are things in the natural that you must correct. Let's look at some other things that can minister to your emotions.

Music, especially praise and worship music, will minister to your emotions. One Greek word for "worship" is *therapeuo* which means *to serve, or to heal, restore to health, or cure.* Matthew **8:2-3** gives the account where, *"...there came a leper and worshiped him, saying, Lord, if thou wilt, thou canst make me clean. And Jesus put forth his hand, and touched him saying, I will; be thou clean. And immediately his leprosy was cleansed."* As you worship God, you will activate His healing power not just for your physical body, but also for your soul.

Saul was troubled by an evil spirit, tormented with depression and fear, and could not sleep. He kept David in his service to play the harp whenever the evil spirit troubled him. He was soothed and found relief by David's music.

But the Spirit of the Lord had left Saul, and instead, the Lord had sent a tormenting spirit that filled him with depression and fear... And whenever the tormenting spirit

from God troubled Saul, David would play the harp and Saul would feel better, and the evil spirit would go away.
(1 Samuel 16:14,23 TLB)

Getting into the presence of God will minister to your soul. **Psalms 16:11** tells us that, *"...in thy presence is fullness of joy; at thy right hand are pleasures for evermore."* Wonderful benefits are found in an atmosphere that is saturated with the presence of God. This is where the life and health of God can flow freely through your whole being, touching and ministering to every part of your being as needed.

You can enter into the presence of God in various ways. Sometimes you do this by reading and speaking the Word, sometimes it is through worship and praise. Other times you pour your heart out to God in prayer, many times with tears and weeping **(Psalms 30:5b, Psalms 126:5)**.

Nature can also provide therapeutic value for the emotions. It is significant that when God created man, He put him in a garden instead of a building. The following excerpt is from Robert Schuler's book entitled POWER THOUGHTS.

"...the human being was designed to live in a garden. That's our natural habitat. And if we are moved out of the garden we will adjust downward in order to survive. Put us in a place where there is concrete, asphalt, power poles, sirens, squealing brakes, sounds of yelling and gunfire, and we will lose our profound deep inner tranquility and peace. At that point we will not hear the 'still, small voice of God.' And we will become deviant. The result? Doubters instead of believers. Doubt is an abnormality. Faith is a normality."[1]

The first several verses in **Psalms 23** reveal the impact nature can have on your soul. Ask God to give you some "**Psalms 23:1-3** experiences."

Psalms 23:1, *"The Lord is my shepherd, I shall not want."*
When you come in contact with the grandeur and awesomeness
of nature, it will help you realize how big God really is. **Matthew
6:30** tells us, *"Wherefore, if God so clothe the grass of the
field, which to day is, and to morrow is cast into the oven,
shall be not much more clothe you, O ye of little faith?"*
God has literally provided everything that is necessary for
man's existence.

Psalms 23:2, *"He maketh me to lie down in green
pastures. He leadeth me beside the still waters."* Notice that
God "makes" you lie down in green pastures. God brings us into
a place of rest, peace, and abundance, not into barren and
desolate places. Rest and peace are essential to your well-being.
Being in a peaceful environment surrounded by the tranquility
of nature can have a tremendous healing effect upon your soul.

Psalms 23:3, *"He restoreth my soul: He leadeth me in the
paths of righteousness."* The word "restoreth" is translated
from the Hebrew word *shuwb* which means *to turn back,
retreat, recover, relieve, refresh, rescue, retrieve, or return to
the starting point.* Restoration in your soul can be maximized as
the handiwork of God surrounds you. Everywhere you look you
can see God, for nature represents the Creator. The Creator is
also your Healer.

Often in the "busy-ness" of life people unintentionally go
astray from the righteous paths of God. Pressures, schedules,
circumstances, relationships, and stress are all a part of the fast
paced lifestyles in our society. Without the correct priorities
from the Word of God, the goal of accomplishing things can
really mess up people's thinking.

Peter warns that just going after fleshly or material things
instead of after the righteous things of God will have a negative
effect upon the soul. *"...abstain from fleshly lusts, which war
against the soul."* (1 Peter 2:11). God knows you need to get
away from those things so you can get a proper perspective of

what is really right in the eyes of God. If your priorities are not correct, your mind can become a "war zone."

I remember a time when we went through a period of great difficulty in the ministry. To make a long story short, we found ourselves in rural Florida, living in a small house trailer beside a pond of water, and surrounded by huge pine trees.

The first thing I noticed was the quietness and solitude there. Often the loudest thing we heard was the wind whistling through the pine trees. It seemed as if we were in a world of our own, locked away from the hustle and bustle of the outside world. It took several days to adjust to the serenity and solitude of nature around me.

God took me to a scripture in **Psalms 46:10**, *"Be still, and know that I am God."* Most people are afraid to get quiet because of what they might find out about themselves. But in the quietness and solitude of nature, I found God revealing Himself to me and ministering to me over and over again.

Yes, God spoke to me in my spirit, but He also ministered to me through the natural setting I was in. Often the quietness of my surroundings would come stealing over my soul and the presence of God's peace would engulf me until my soul was in a state of joy and serenity. We stayed there for almost a year until God got me into a place where I had once again found the hope of my calling restored to me.

Other things that will minister to your soul include humor and laughter **(Proverbs 17:22)**, hobbies or recreation, and physical exercise. Physical exercise can help stimulate your blood circulation to your brain. It also helps provide fresh oxygen because you breathe deeper when you exert physical energy.

Different things work for different people, Look for things that will minister to your soul and emotions such as (1) things that cause a break in your daily routine (2) things that give relief from the pressures of life (3) things that produce peace of mind, and (4) things that make you feel good about yourself.

However, one thing that will always minister to your emotions is the Word of God. Nothing can take the place of the Word of God in ministering to your soul. Reading, believing, and speaking the Word of God will have a healing effect upon your soul.

CAUSES FOR EMOTIONAL PROBLEMS

Two primary causes of emotional problems are (1) failure to receive forgiveness, and (2) failure to give forgiveness. If you harbor unforgiveness in your spirit, you will have problems in your soul. You will think wrong thoughts. Emotionally, you may respond to life's problems the wrong way.

I know people who refused to forgive those who didn't treat them right, and I watched them go through mental and emotional problems. Attitudes of resentment, bitterness, fear, and being critical showed up in their lives and guilt, condemnation, and a sense of unworthiness prevailed. Some became very controlling and manipulative in relationships to make sure that what had happened in the past would not happen again.

As this process continued these people seemed to lose the ability to distinguish between actual facts and their perception of things. The Word of God was no longer the absolute governing factor in their lives. They used only the portion of the Word of God that justified their position, or that applied to the other person.

Some of those people contracted physical diseases such as cancer or arthritis. Many physical diseases have inroads into the lives of people because of their spiritual and soulish condition.

Some people readily forgive others but won't forgive themselves. They are harder on themselves than God is. But

Matthew 22:39 reveals that you are to love both others and yourself. *"...Thou shalt love thy neighbor as thyself."*

The devil brings up things in your past with which to torment you, even if you have already applied the blood of Jesus Christ and asked God to forgive you of these things. But you must believe the Word of God no matter what the devil tells you. **Romans 3:4** declares, *"...let God be true, but every man a liar..."* This means you must choose to believe what the Word of God tells you rather than what you are experiencing, or what the devil is telling you.

Your symptoms will change if you continue to believe the Word of God. **1 John 1:9** assures us that, *"If we confess our sins, he is faithful and just to forgive us our sins, and to cleanse us from all unrighteousness."* Believe what **1 John 1:9** tells you rather than letting the devil torment you with his accusations and lies.

There are other causes for emotional problems such as demonic influence, perverted sex, and abusive relationships, but the answers to all these problems are found in the Word of God.

EVIDENCE OF DAMAGED EMOTIONS

When do you need God to help you with your emotions? How can you tell if you really have a problem in this area?

Sometimes people need help in realizing what is not healthy. Some people have been in unhealthy situations all their lives and they don't even realize it. A person may not be aware of his need to be whole, or that God wants to help him get to a place of being whole. He may have been in this condition so long that he thinks this is normal.

Dr. David Seamonds offers the following list as evidence of damaged emotions:[2] (1) having a severe or continual sense of unworthiness (2) being a perfectionist (3) being supersensitive, or "wearing your feelings on your sleeve" (4) being continually fearful; the greatest is probably fear of failure (5) perverted sex, which can also cause damaged emotions.

Dr. Seamonds also asks several questions to help determine if problems exist that need to be dealt with. Is there resentment in your heart toward those who apparently caused this? Do you really love those who did this? Is there still resentment rising up in you when their names are mentioned or when you meet them? Has the blood of Christ cleansed your spirit, or are you still harboring unforgiveness toward others, or toward yourself? Are you being truthful about this situation, and to yourself? Have you accepted responsibility for what happened, and for your present condition?

You can have victory in the area of your emotions, but you must understand the rules that apply to having a healthy soul. As you study the Word of God, and then believe what it tells you, you can speak the Word of God to your difficulties and triumph over them.

POINTS TO PONDER

1. LIST SOME THINGS THAT MINISTER TO THE EMOTIONS.

2. LIST SOME CAUSES AND EVIDENCES OF DAMAGED EMOTIONS.

3. ASK YOURSELF THESE THREE QUESTIONS TO DETERMINE THE STATE OF YOUR EMOTIONS. ASK GOD TO HELP YOU DEAL WITH THESE THINGS.

(1) DO I STILL RESENT THOSE WHO APPARENTLY CAUSED THIS?

(2) DO I STILL REACT TOWARD THESE PEOPLE WHEN I'M REMINDED OF THEM?

(3) DO I TAKE RESPONSIBILITY FOR WHAT HAPPENED?

Chapter 10

JESUS IS YOUR HEALER

Seeing then that we have a great high priest,
that is passed into the heavens, Jesus the
Son of God, let us hold fast our profession.
For we have not an high priest which cannot be
touched with the feeling of our infirmities; but was
in all points tempted like as we are, yet without sin.
Let us therefore come boldly unto the throne of
grace, that we may obtain mercy, and find grace to
help in time of need.
(Hebrews 4:14-16)

JESUS, YOUR HIGH PRIEST, KNOWS THE FEELINGS OF YOUR INFIRMITIES

The Word of God states that Jesus knows your human weaknesses and frailties. Jesus became a man who walked upon this earth like you and me. You can look at His life and study what Paul wrote in his epistles to understand what to do with your weaknesses and frailties.

The word "infirmities" used in **Hebrews 4:15** stems from the Greek word *asthenia*, and refers to *feebleness (of body or mind), by implication, malady, moral frailty, disease, sickness, or weakness.* Though infirmities (weaknesses) are not sins they can undermine our resistance to temptation. They may cause you to be inclined to sin, sometimes without a conscious choice on your part. This may apply to areas in which your resistance is weak. That is why **Hebrews 12:1** admonishes you to, *"...lay aside every weight, and the sin which doth so easily beset us, and let us run with patience the race that is set before us."*

Jesus is not only touched with the *fact* (the crippling, the weakness, the emotional hang-ups and the inner conflicts) of your infirmities, but He also understands the *feelings* (the frustrations, anxiety, depression, hurts, rejection, loneliness) of your infirmities. This word "feeling" in **Hebrews 4:15** comes from the Greek word *"sumpatheo"* meaning *to feel sympathy with, have compassion with, to be touched with the feeling of,* or *"fellow feeling."*

Matthew 12:20, in referring to Jesus, said, *"a bruised reed He shall not break, and smoking flax shall He not quench..."* Jesus was moved with compassion for the people, and healed them. He straightened and strengthened those who were like bruised reeds instead of breaking them off and discarding them. Jesus breathed life and healing upon those whose life was like smoking flax until they were burning brightly again. Jesus cares for you as you go through this life.

JESUS' EXPERIENCES ALLOW HIM TO IDENTIFY WITH YOUR EXPERIENCES

Who in the days of his flesh, when he had offered up prayers and supplications with strong crying and tears unto him that was able to save him from death, and was heard in that he feared;

Though he were a Son, yet learned he obedience by the things which he suffered;

(Hebrews 5:7-8)

Nothing you can experience is outside the perimeters of what Jesus experienced while He was upon this earth. Jesus experienced torment and agony in His soul in the Garden of Gethsemane *"My soul is exceeding sorrowful, even unto death"* (Matthew 26:37,38). Judas Iscariot betrayed him. *"But Jesus said unto him, Judas, betrayest thou the Son of Man with a kiss?"* (Luke 22:48). He was forsaken by all. *"Peter,*

What, could you not watch with Me for one hour?" (Matthew 26:40). *"...all the disciples forsook Him, and fled"* (Matthew 26:56).

Jesus endured false accusations and mockery at His trial. *"Then did they spit in his face, and buffeted him; and others smote Him with the palms of their hands"* (Matthew 26:67).

Jesus was mocked and forsaken on the cross. *"If thou be the Son of God come down from the cross"* (Matthew 27:40). *"My God, my God, why hast thou forsaken me?"* (Matthew 27:46).

Not only did Jesus suffer during His physical life, but He also was made sin for us at the cross (2 Corinthians 5:21). The cross is a major point of God identifying with man. Because of this, Jesus knows how sin feels, along with the guilt, condemnation, and unworthiness that comes with it.

...let us also lay aside every encumbrance, and the sin which so easily entangles us, and let us run with endurance the race that is set before us,

fixing our eyes on Jesus, the author and perfecter of faith, who for the joy set before Him endured the cross, despising the shame, and has sat down at the right hand of the throne of God.

For consider Him who has endured such hostility by sinners against Himself, so that you may not grow weary and lose heart.

(Hebrews 12:1-3, NASB)

Remember that whatever you're experiencing is not unfamiliar to Jesus. He has suffered far beyond the depth that any other person has or ever will suffer. *However, not only did Jesus identify with mankind at Calvary through what He suffered, He in turn made it possible for man to identify with Him in His resurrection from the dead and in His victory over Satan, sin, and every other evil power!*

JESUS' VICTORY IS YOUR VICTORY

Seeing then that we have a great high priest, that is passed into the heavens, Jesus the Son of God, let us hold fast our profession.

For we have not a high priest which cannot be touched with the feeling of our infirmities; but was in all points tempted like as we are, yet without sin.

Let us therefore come boldly unto the throne of grace, that we may obtain mercy, and find grace to help in time of need.
(Hebrews 4:14-16)

What Jesus endured at the cross you do not have to bear. The work of redemption was a vicarious work. Jesus did it for others, not for Himself. Therefore, you can identify with Christ in the victory He obtained and apply it to your life.

Did Jesus endure the cross? Did Jesus finish His work in spite of all the suffering He went through? Did Jesus defeat the devil, death, and the grave, rising up in His glory to ascend to the right hand of the Father? The answer to all these questions is a big resounding, "YES!"

How then can you apply the victory of Jesus Christ into your life? **Number one**, continually confess with your mouth what Jesus did for you at Calvary, who you are in Christ, and what the Word of God has promised to you. Continually confessing or speaking what the Word of God says in these three areas will help you more than almost anything else you can do. Confess what God has said in His Word rather than your failures, feelings, or experiences.

I am convinced that if we could just get people to say what the Word of God says about them rather than just talking about their problems, many of their problems would be solved. Identify yourself with Christ rather than with your problems. Who you are, and what you have in Christ is greater than any problem you are going through. There are many scriptures,

72

especially in the letters written by the Apostle Paul, that tells you who you are in Christ. This is your real identity as a Christian.

For example, **2 Corinthians 5:17** tells us, *"Therefore if any man be in Christ, he is a new creature: old things are passed away; behold, all things are become new."* Begin to confess you are a new creature in Christ, old things are passed away, and now you are living a new life in Christ Jesus. This will affect every area of your spirit, soul, and body.

Number two, realize Jesus is your high priest, and He identifies with what you are experiencing. You can always come to Him with your problems. Jesus is interceding and praying for you. He will stand by you, strengthen you, and see you through.

Jesus also sent the Holy Spirit to guide you into the Word of God so you can know what Jesus did for you. God has established a New Covenant with you that offers love instead of judgment, mercy instead of requiring sacrifice, and grace instead of the law.

Number three, come boldly to the throne of grace. You can find mercy and help in time of need. But, someone might say, "It was my fault. I'm in this condition because of what I did. I don't deserve any help."

That may be true, but did you notice where God told you to come to? The throne of grace! The throne of unmerited favor! The place of acceptance! You may not deserve it but God has extended His grace toward you anyway. If it were on the basis of what you deserve, it would cease to be grace.

This means you do not come to God for help based on your own works; you come to God based on the work of Jesus at Calvary! You come based upon the punishment and sin He bore for you on the cross. His suffering has opened the door for your well-being!

Jesus did not need the victory at Calvary for himself; Jesus had the victory before He ever came to the earth. The victory Jesus obtained at Calvary was for you! Now you are to claim that victory, healing, deliverance, safety, and well-being as yours in Jesus' Name.

This means before you came to the throne of grace for help you may have been bothered by, *"...every weight, and the sin which doth so easily beset us..."* (Hebrews 12:1). But after you have received His grace and strength, the weight is gone, and the sin that so easily beset you can no longer do so!

You may have come to the throne of grace with sickness and disease in your body, but you can go away from the throne of grace having received the healing Jesus provided for you at Calvary. You may come to God discouraged, depressed, and having no hope. Maybe you are rejected and betrayed, and suffered bitterness and loneliness. But after you receive grace and forgiveness, you can go your way, shouting and rejoicing because Jesus has obtained the victory for you.

POINTS TO PONDER

1. JESUS IS NOT ONLY TOUCHED WITH THE FACT BUT HE ALSO UNDERSTANDS THE FEELINGS OF YOUR INFIRMITIES.

2. JESUS' EXPERIENCES ALLOW HIM TO IDENTIFY WITH YOUR EXPERIENCES.

3. THE VICTORY THAT JESUS OBTAINED AT CALVARY WAS FOR YOU AND ME.

4. HOW DOES THIS HELP YOU WALK THROUGH YOUR HARDSHIPS?

Chapter 11

THINKING THE THOUGHTS OF GOD

But as it is written, Eye hath not seen, nor ear heard,
neither have entered into the heart of man, the things
which God hath prepared for them that love him.
But God hath revealed them unto us by his Spirit; for the
Spirit searcheth all things, yea, the deep things of God.
Now we have received, not the spirit of the world, but the
spirit which is of God; that we might know the things that
are freely given to us of God.
(1 Corinthians 2:9-10,12)

As you read and meditate upon the Word of God, you open your thinking to God's thoughts. The Bible is full of "God-thoughts." You can know the thoughts of God because He has written them in His Word for you.

Thinking the thoughts of God doesn't mean you have to know every detail or figure out in your mind what God wants to do. But we do need to know as much of God's Word as we can, and maintain a mind that is teachable and willing to adjust to the thoughts of God as they are revealed to us.

Knowing the thoughts of God's Word will enable you to set your affections on things above and flow with the direction of the Holy Spirit. Then you can move in the direction God wants you to go. Mark Hankins said, *"Your affections will determine your direction."*[1]

Many people have trouble doing what the Holy Ghost tells them to do because they have not taken time to hear the written Word of God until it becomes the dominant thought pattern in their thinking; their thoughts are about other things – perhaps the things of the world, current events, or the weather.

Bob Harrison said, *"When God speaks, your mind is your greatest enemy."*[2] Often when God speaks, He shares thoughts that are far beyond the thoughts you have been thinking. When a new thought is presented, the mind tries to relate it to other thoughts with which it has already received. When no existing thoughts are found to connect the new thought, the mind wants to reject it, and say the thought is not true.

For example, your mind may have a hard time seeing how an event that happened 2,000 years ago could affect the destiny of mankind today, but **John 3:16** tells us that Christ at Calvary provided salvation to all who believe on Him.

It's the same way with healing. The first time you read **Isaiah 53:5,** *"...by His stripes you are healed,"* your mind may have said, "I'm sick - can't you see I'm sick? What do you mean - by His stripes I'm healed?" When a person is confronted with the truth of **Isaiah 53:5**, his mind tries to relate it to other thoughts it knows about healing, and if no other thoughts are found, the mind wants to reject **Isaiah 53:5** and say, "It can't be true."

Some people have trouble relating to **Malachi 3:10-12** concerning tithing and giving offerings. In math class at school, you weren't taught that when you subtracted, a multiplication process would begin. But God says if you will subtract a tenth from your income He will multiply what is left until you have more than what you started with. The mind tries to find existing thoughts to which it can connect **Malachi 3:10-12**. If it can't find any, the mind wants to reject the thoughts concerning tithes and offerings as untrue.

It is necessary to renew your mind with the Word of God. As you do, you are building new files in your mind. After awhile, when a truth from the Word of God comes into your mind, the mind will not fight it anymore because it recognizes it as true. This is how you put thoughts of God into your mind and begin thinking them.

KNOWING THE THOUGHTS OF GOD

For my thoughts are not your thoughts, neither are your ways my ways, saith the Lord. For as the heavens are higher than the earth, so are my ways higher than your ways, and my thoughts than your thoughts.
(Isaiah 55:8-9)

Some people think you cannot know the thoughts of God. However, God has written His thoughts in a book called the Bible so you can learn them. The context of **Isaiah 55:8-9** shows that God was speaking to people who were not born again. It is true that the natural, sinful man doesn't have the same thoughts God does, nor can he walk in God's ways.

But even under the old Covenant, God made His ways known to Moses **(Psalms 103:7)**, and in the New Covenant you have a better covenant established upon better promises!

As a believer, you have the Holy Spirit living in you. One of the things the Holy Spirit does is reveal to you the Word of God, which are the thoughts of God in written form. *You can know the thoughts and the ways of God by reading His Word.*

Paul said in **Romans 11:33,** *"O the depth of the riches both of the wisdom and knowledge of God! how unsearchable are his judgments, and his ways past finding out!"* You will embark on an unending journey to find new thoughts and discover new ways God has of doing things. God is willing that you should find out as much as you can. It is possible for believers to know what God is thinking.

DISCOVERING THE THINGS OF GOD

The things of God are waiting to be discovered. God has put them where they can be found. *The key to finding the things of God is a renewed mind that will flow with the revelation the Holy Spirit gives from the Word of God.*

I remember as a young Christian, I went through a period of time when it seemed as if I could not comprehend anything I read in the Bible. I became very frustrated, and almost stopped reading my Bible.

One night I went to church to hear a guest speaker whom I had never met. At the end of his message he pointed to me and said, "Don't try to figure out what the Bible means. Your job is to read it, and trust the Holy Spirit to reveal it to you." This revolutionized my Bible reading and I opened my thinking to embrace what the Holy Spirit would show me. I began to read the Word of God, anticipating the revelation the Holy Spirit would bring to me.

At that time, I worked in a factory, doing things which didn't require a lot of mental concentration. As I worked I would meditate on the scriptures I had read. Revelation by the Holy Spirit came so freely that frequently I would have to stop and write down what I learned.

The Holy Spirit reveals the things of God. He reveals the Word of God to you. God has many things for you including both spiritual and material things. As you renew your mind to the Word of God you can hear the voice of the Holy Spirit more easily and in a greater measure.

God wants you to think supernatural thoughts; the Holy Spirit will say and do things that are supernatural. As you renew your mind to God's thoughts and ways, you can enter into a higher realm of flowing with God than ever before.

MOVING WITH THE HOLY GHOST

There is a great outpouring of God's Spirit in the earth in these days, and it is happening in a greater measure than ever before. This is what the prophets have foretold! God is looking for people who will cooperate with His Spirit in this present day move; people who want to move with Him, think they can move with Him, and dare to move with Him!

You will flow with the Holy Ghost according to your thinking and understanding of the Word of God. You can increase your effectiveness of moving with the Holy Ghost by renewing your mind with the thoughts of God's Word.

The Word of God will reveal the Holy Spirit to you. Jesus shared insight about the Holy Spirit in **John 14-16**. You can know the person of the Holy Spirit. As you know the Word of God and the person of the Holy Spirit, you can move in greater dimensions of the supernatural. Then your thoughts will reflect the work of God rather than your own efforts.

Many Christians desire to be a vessel through which the gifts of the Holy Spirit can flow. The Holy Spirit wants to move through everyone who will allow Him to do so. Why then are there so few Christians being used as vessels through which the gifts and power of the Holy Spirit flow? *Primarily, it's because people think they can't.* They do not think they know how, or they think they don't know the voice of the Holy Spirit well enough to operate in the gifts of the Spirit.

The biggest hindrance in flowing with the Holy Spirit is your thinking. Often, when God reveals the big plans He has for people, they reject them because of their thinking. Stanley Jones said, *"The chief way that you and I are disloyal to Christ is when we make small what He intended to make large."*[3]

*Now unto him that is able to do exceeding abundantly
above all that we ask or think, according to the power that
worketh in us,*

(Ephesians 3:20)

The church has relegated this verse onto the sovereignty of
God far too long. This verse has been quoted with the idea that
"if God wants to He will someway, somewhere, somehow,
someday, with somebody." The church has sat passively by
telling each other, "God is able to do exceeding, abundantly
above what we can think or ask!"

Yet God has told you exactly how much He will work in your
life. Yes, it is true that God is ABLE to do abundantly above all
that you ask or think, but that doesn't mean He WILL do
abundantly above all that you ask or think. Notice this verse
says that God will do, *"...ACCORDING to the power that
worketh in you."*

What then is the governing factor determining how the power
of God will work in you? *Your thinking and your asking
determines how the power of God works in and through you.*
When you think God's thoughts you will speak words in line
with the Word of God, and this will allow the power of God to
work effectually in and through you.

The Holy Spirit is always listening to what you think and ask.
He is waiting for you to speak words that will release Him to
work in your life. He wants to do great and mighty things in you,
and move you into a realm of living that you desire.

IN THE MIDST OF THE GLORY OF GOD

*And I will shake all the nations, and the desire of all
nations shall come: and I will fill this house with glory, saith
the Lord of hosts.*

The silver is mine, and the gold is mine, saith the Lord of hosts.

The glory of this latter house shall be greater than that of the former, saith the Lord of hosts: and in this place will I give peace, saith the Lord of hosts.

(Haggai 2:7-9)

The easiest place to think the thoughts of God and ask God for the right things for your life is in His glory. **Haggai 2:7-9** states that God will give you thoughts of plenty and thoughts of peace in His glory, no matter what you may be experiencing in your life.

Notice in the verses above that in the midst of talking about His glory, God also talks about gold and silver. This is actually a picture of heaven, where there are streets of gold in the midst of the presence of God! God wants the same thing to happen on earth. Get into the glory of God and receive a revelation of God's abundance that will cause you to move on up even when others are failing and going down.

The Apostle Paul is one of the greatest examples of a person who was changed in the glory of God. His thoughts about the things of God were changed in a moment when the glory of God came upon him on the Damascus Road **(Acts 9:3-8)**. He stopped thinking thoughts of murder, hatred, and of persecuting Christians and began thinking thoughts about fulfilling the will of God.

Often, the biggest hindrance to flowing with the plan of God is found in your thought life. Remember that people will flow with the Holy Spirit according to their understanding, or the knowledge they have, so the glory of God becomes invaluable as a change agent for your thought life.

But we all, with open face beholding as in a glass the glory of the Lord, are changed into the same image from

glory to glory, even as by the Spirit of the Lord.
(2 Corinthians 3:18)

As you enter into God's glory, He will take away your old, earthly, worldly thoughts and give you thoughts of His kingdom, power, and glory. Your priorities will change. Things deemed important in the earth may not be important in the glory of God. In His glory you can have your mind expanded to embrace His thoughts and learn to flow with the Holy Spirit. Let the Holy Spirit help you change your thoughts so you can move up into what God has for you!

POINTS TO PONDER

1. AS YOU READ AND MEDITATE UPON THE WORD OF GOD, YOU OPEN YOUR THINKING TO GOD'S THOUGHTS.

2. IT IS POSSIBLE FOR BELIEVERS TO KNOW WHAT GOD IS THINKING.

3. YOU CAN INCREASE YOUR EFFECTIVENESS OF MOVING WITH THE HOLY GHOST BY RENEWING YOUR MIND WITH THE THOUGHTS OF GOD'S WORD.

4. THE BIGGEST HINDRANCE IN FLOWING WITH THE HOLY SPIRIT IS YOUR THINKING.

Chapter 12

THOUGHTS OF FAITH

HARMONY BETWEEN
YOUR SOUL & SPIRIT

Rev. Kenneth Hagin said, *"Our thinking must be in line with the Word of God, because we cannot believe beyond the actual knowledge we have of God's Word."*[1] Developing a prosperous soul does not take the place of having faith in God's Word. Rather, it helps you to have strong faith in God's Word.

It is possible for the human spirit to be enlightened on the things of God without the human soul possessing understanding. A person can have faith in his heart, and doubt in his head. While a person may be in this condition, it certainly isn't God's best. God desires that your soul and your spirit be in agreement, and have knowledge and understanding of the things of God.

God desires your soul and spirit to be in harmony with His Word. This will help you to have strong faith in God. The Holy Spirit wants to enlighten both your spirit and your soul by the Word of God. Your spirit receives revelation from the Holy Spirit, while your soul is renewed day by day through the Word of God. God desires your spirit and your soul to be in agreement by having the same revelation. E. W. Kenyon stated, *"We find that as soon as we can bring perfect assurance that the disease was laid on Christ, and the mind comes into agreement with the spirit, healing is inevitable."*[2]

The value of a prosperous soul can be experienced when perfect harmony exists between soul and spirit because they both receive their enlightenment according to the Word of God. Then you can experience peace, and express great faith in God's Word.

The soul is the "gate" to the heart; knowledge in the soul comes before faith in the heart does. **Romans 10:17** states that, *"...faith cometh by hearing, and hearing by the Word of God."* As you fill your mind with the knowledge of God's Word, the Holy Spirit will begin to write the Word upon your heart. When the Holy Spirit engraves the Word upon your heart it creates faith in the Word. Your ability to have faith in your heart concerning the Word of God is in direct proportion to the knowledge you have of God's Word.

Rev. Kenneth Hagin said, *"What we believe is a result of our thinking. If we think wrong, we will believe wrong. If our believing is wrong, our confession will be wrong. In other words, what we say will be wrong. It all hinges on our thinking."*[3] Think thoughts according to God's Word; this is the correct foundation for your faith in God. If your thinking is based upon the world's way of doing things, you have the wrong foundation for faith in God. At some point the pressures of life will cause your incorrect foundation of "worldly thinking" to crumble, and your faith will not be strong enough to withstand the adversities of life and the attacks of the enemy.

MENTAL ASSENT VERSUS HEART FAITH

I am not referring to "mental assent." Just thinking the right thoughts in your mind is not enough, nor is it an end in itself. Some people think that knowledge is all they need, but if that were so, knowledge would be their saviour. The reason we must have knowledge from God's Word is because it will enable us to believe the Word with our hearts. Knowing the thoughts of God helps us to believe right.

Some religious people get upset with the positive mental attitude people, but God is not going to work with negative attitudes! God is always positive toward believers. **Romans 8:32** tells us that God is for us, not against us. Negative thinking isn't an alternative for us.

Positive mental attitude is all right as far as it goes, but there is more to receiving from God than just that. The value of a positive mental attitude is that it is in agreement with the promises of God's Word which you must believe in your heart in order to receive from God **(Mark 11:23-24)**. You may never see the results of believing with your heart until the attitudes of your mind are first in agreement with the Word of God. Remember that the decisions of life are made in the soul, including the decision to walk by faith.

DECIDE TO THINK THOUGHTS OF FAITH

What kind of thoughts does God think? He always thinks thoughts in agreement with His Word. More specifically, He thinks thoughts of faith and love. God always thinks "possibility thoughts." He thinks conquering thoughts, thoughts of victory and not defeat, thoughts of healing and prosperity, thoughts of the harvest of souls and salvation.

Make a decision to think thoughts from God's Word. Guard your thought life so that only thoughts of faith in God dwell in your soul. Be quick to eject thoughts that do not express faith.

Recently someone sent me a cassette tape of a message they had preached. I listened to it for a few minutes, and suddenly up out of my spirit I said, "That's not faith!" I ejected the tape from the tape player and threw it away. *I refuse to allow thoughts contrary to faith in God's Word to occupy my mind.*

Many Christians have not filled their minds and hearts with God's thoughts. Therefore they have a difficult time believing God's Word. They waver between thoughts of God's Word and thoughts of this world. They want to believe the Word but because they have not taken the time to put the Word in them, they are still moved by what goes on around them.

Fill your mind and heart with God's thoughts from His Word that tells you all things are possible. Continually dwell upon God's Word that says you're a conqueror in life. When the challenges of life come, those possibility thoughts and conquering thoughts you have put in your soul and heart will rise up and govern your steps. They will guide you to victory! They will enable you to see God's promises come to pass.

Dwell upon the promises of God in your soul and spirit until they rise up strong within you. Let them cause a spirit of faith to rise up in you that will not be denied. A spirit of faith declares it is possible to conquer the mountains that appear in your life. Trouble may come, and storm clouds may appear on the horizon, but they are no match for the spirit of faith that rises up on the inside of you and dares to think, believe, and speak the Word of God no matter what it may look like.

Let the possibilities of God begin to dwell richly in you. **Mark 10:27** declares that *"...with God all things are possible."* Meditate upon this fact that ALL things are possible. In God there is no defeat. In God there is no such thing as failure. Begin to imagine God working all things for your good **(Romans 8:28)**. Jesus said, *"If thou canst believe, all things are possible to him that believeth."* (Mark 9:23).

When the angel told Mary that she would conceive by the Holy Ghost, and that she would give birth to the Son of God, her response was not one of unbelief. Although she did not see how this would be possible, she immediately responded, *"...be it unto me according to thy word"* (Luke 1:38). When Jesus was born and the shepherds came and told of the angelic visitation they had concerning the Son of God, **Luke 2:19** said Mary *"kept all these and pondered them in her heart."* This reveals a pattern of responding in faith to God's Word.

Decide that whether you understand what God is saying or not, your immediate response will be, "Be it unto me according to thy Word." Then take the things God has spoken to you and begin to ponder them in your heart and mind. Meditate upon them until the revelation of God's Word comes to you and you rise up in faith to accomplish what has been spoken to you in the power of the Holy Ghost. God will see your faith and say to you, "Be it unto you according to your faith!"

RIGHT THINKING HELPS FAITH'S CONFESSION

It is impossible to maintain a strong confession of faith while continually thinking thoughts of doubt. You must learn to control your thoughts by "recording" new thoughts from God's Word. Start reading the Word, or listen to tapes of messages on faith.

Don't allow your mind to "play back" any old thoughts that come along. Put new thoughts in your mind from the Word instead of dwelling on your problems.

You see, the real problem people experience when they have trouble confessing the Word is that they either don't control their thought lives, or they don't listen to the Word of God enough until they believe it. *Faith's confession is designed to come up out of the overflow of the Word that is in your heart.*

I know there are crisis times in our lives when our minds are overwhelmed, and seem to go into shock. In moments like this it takes great effort to make a confession of faith, or even think thoughts of faith. That's why you need to control your thoughts and feed upon the Word of God when there is no crisis in your life. Don't wait for trouble to come knocking on your door before you decide to control your thoughts and listen to the Word. That's like trying to stop the water from flowing over the dam after it breaks!

Remember what Rev. Kenneth Hagin said, *"What we believe is a result of our thinking. If we think wrong, we will believe wrong. If our believing is wrong, our confession will be wrong. In other words, what we say will be wrong. It all hinges on our thinking."*[3]

Realize that you must get your thinking right so that you can believe right, and so that your confession will be right. Then you'll have what you need from God.

POINTS TO PONDER

1. HARMONY BETWEEN SOUL AND SPIRIT WILL HELP YOU HAVE STRONG FAITH IN GOD.

2. YOUR ABILITY TO HAVE FAITH IN YOUR HEART CONCERNING THE WORD OF GOD IS IN DIRECT PROPORTION TO THE KNOWLEDGE YOU HAVE OF GOD'S WORD.

3. THINKING THOUGHTS ACCORDING TO GOD'S WORD IS THE CORRECT FOUNDATION FOR YOUR FAITH IN GOD.

4. GUARD YOUR THOUGHT LIFE SO THAT ONLY THOUGHTS OF FAITH IN GOD DWELL IN YOUR SOUL.

Chapter 13

BREAKING INTO NEW REALMS

For my thoughts are not your thoughts, neither are your ways my ways, saith the Lord. For as the heavens are higher than the earth, so are my ways higher than your ways, and my thoughts than your thoughts.
(Isaiah 55:8-9)

God's thoughts are different than man's thoughts because they are thoughts of another realm. God's thoughts are not only different but also higher than man's thoughts. They reflect the spirit realm of God, which has greater powers and higher purposes than the earthly realm in which man lives.

However, it is possible for you to know what God is thinking. When you know what God's Word says about a certain situation, you know the thoughts of God concerning that situation. God's thoughts are always in agreement with His Word. Anyone can learn the thoughts of God if they want to. God has written them in the Bible so you can know them.

EVERY REALM HAS ITS OWN THOUGHTS

One day I was meditating on the Word as I was going to preach at a church, and God shared with me that every realm has its own thoughts. God's realm has thoughts according to His Word. Man's realm has thoughts dictated by the limitations of its physical environment. Satan's realm has demonic thoughts that are against God, man, and all that is good.

This is why the world doesn't understand the things of God. It's why poor people do not understand riches. The chronically sick person often does not comprehend the realm of health. This reveals why there is conflict between employers and employees. Every realm has its own thoughts.

Racial problems have their roots in this fact. This doesn't mean that any particular race is correct and others aren't, but they do think differently. I like what one minister friend of mine said: *"One of the signs of maturity in Christ is that you can appreciate the diversity of people who are under the common cause of Christ."* Let's recognize the strength and weaknesses of one another, be unified under the blood of Christ, and work together to win the world to Jesus Christ.

Several years ago I was preaching the gospel in several former communist countries in Eastern Europe which now have a democratic government. While these countries were under communist rule, the government made decisions for the people, but under the present democratic government, the same people are on their own, and make their own choices of where to live and work, and what lifestyle they want.

The attitudes and ways of many of these people still reflect the possibilities and limitations determined by the former communist government. Why is this? Every realm has its own thoughts. A communist government and a democratic society are two different realms. They think differently.

THE FIRST STEP
TO NEW REALMS OF LIFE

In order for these people to go from a lifestyle of being told the government will take care of them to one in which they are on their own they must embrace a major mind shift or change of thinking. Many of these people had difficulty making the change in their thought lives. Even though they are now free to do whatever they chose to do, many are unable to function successfully in an environment in which people make their own choices regarding where to live, their professions, activities, and their lifestyles. In order to experience real freedom, they will have to go through the process of changing their thoughts.

The first step in going to another level or realm is to begin to think the thoughts of that level or realm. A person must be enlightened according to the thoughts of that realm in order to function in it. This is true no matter what realm you want to enter into.

Have you ever gone out of the environment you live in and visited an area you were totally unfamiliar with? A friend of mine who was an artist in New York City told me he could always tell who was new in the city, because they were always looking up at the tall buildings! They were in an environment or culture that was new to them, and did not really know the thoughts of that realm, so they acted differently than those who were functioning there.

To enter into God's realm, you have to begin to think thoughts found in God's Word. As you receive God's thoughts from His Word, the Holy Spirit will begin to change your thinking. Begin to imagine and meditate upon those thoughts. As you keep those thoughts in front of you, you will be able to eventually believe them, say them, and do them. As you think the thoughts of another level or realm, you will begin to comprehend the benefits, and a desire to go there begins to stir within your soul.

Let's see how this works in the realm of prosperity. It is a proven fact that rich people think differently than poor people do. Therefore, if you want to go from poverty to prosperity you must learn the thoughts of the realm of prosperity.

Unless you change your thought patterns and the level of the knowledge you have about money, you will never rise to a higher level of wealth than where you are right now.

You may receive a large sum of money, but unless you change your thinking about money, you will return to the financial condition you're presently in. Why is this? The decisions of life, including what to do with money, are made in the soul. The ability to keep and use money wisely comes with thinking the right thoughts concerning prosperity. You must first change your thoughts about prosperity so that money will be a blessing to you.

Here's another example. If a sick person wishes to enter the realm of health he must change his thoughts with the healing promises from the Word of God. Many people lose their healing because they never take the time to change their thoughts to what God's Word reveals about healing.

It is possible for a person to be ignorant of the thoughts in the realm of healing, and still receive healing through a special manifestation of the Holy Spirit. But that person may not know enough to keep the devil from stealing his health. If a person changes his thinking so that it agrees with the healing promises of God's Word, he will be able to enjoy good health.

In the realm of business, employees must change their thinking if they want to enter into a management position or become an employer because they are entering into another realm. They must make the adjustment in their thought lives from being followers to becoming managers or leaders.

THE ISRAELITES GO TO A NEW LAND

All the commandments which I command thee this day shall ye observe to do, that ye may live, and multiply, and

*go in and possess the land which the Lord sware unto your
fathers.*

*And thou shalt remember all the way which the Lord thy
God led thee these forty years in the wilderness, to humble
thee, and to prove thee, to know what was in thine heart,
whether thou wouldest keep his commandments, or no.*

(Deuteronomy 8:1,2)

Notice in these verses that the reason God took forty years to
take the Israelites into the Promised Land was to humble them
and prove them so they would know what was in their hearts.
*God had to change their hearts and minds to His way of
thinking in order for them to possess the Promised Land.*

It took time for God to get the Israelites out of Egypt where
they were slaves and in to possess the Promised Land. God had
to change their mentality from slavery to conquering. Slaves
have to change their thinking to become conquerors. Slaves do
not have a "fight to conquer" mentality; they think thoughts of
obedience, and do what they are told.

Slaves do not possess a land because they never decide to
possess it. The possibility of possessing the land is not
entertained in their thoughts. Therefore they remain in
captivity, not because it is impossible for them to be free, but
because they think this is all they can have in life.

You have to think bigger thoughts than the land you want to
possess or the new realm you want to enter into. *It is impossible
for you to enter into a new level of living when the thoughts of
that level overwhelm you.* To be overwhelmed means *to
languish, fail, faint, become feeble, or to hide oneself.* A person
who is overwhelmed is usually reduced to a state of inactivity.
Often the devil comes with a barrage of thoughts to overwhelm
you and keep you from doing anything. He knows if he can win
the battle in your mind, the real battle of possessing what God
has promised will never take place.

When the twelve Israelite spies went into the Promised Land, ten of them were overwhelmed, not by the inhabitants of the land, but by their thoughts of possessing the land. Their own thoughts defeated them. The greatest battles in life are fought in the soul. *If you can win the battle of your thoughts, possessing the actual land God said He has given to you will be easy.*

Except for Joshua and Caleb, the first generation of Israelites who were twenty years and older did not make the adjustment in their thinking. God had to let them die in the wilderness, and then work through the next generation.

COURAGE TO POSSESS THE PROMISED LAND

In **Joshua 1:1-9** Joshua receives instructions from God to enter into the Promised Land. What issue does God emphasize the most during this conversation? Three times God tells Joshua, *"be strong and of a good courage"* (Joshua 1:6-7,9).

Not only do you need physical strength to possess the land; you also need courage in your heart and mind. Most people quit and never enter into what God has for them, not because of a lack of physical strength, but because of a lack of courage. Courageous thoughts come from God and His Word. *"Courage comes when the cause is greater than the circumstances."*[1] (Gerald Brooks).

2 Corinthians 4:16 says, *"For which cause we faint not..."* Many people faint and quit because they (1) have no cause or (2) forget their cause. You'll find your cause by fellowshipping with God. What does God speak to you during this time? What is it that burns strong within your heart? Let whatever God speaks to your heart become your cause.

Meditate upon the things God puts in your heart until you are consumed with them. Ponder these things within you until your soul burns white-hot with the desire to go there and do it. Embrace the thoughts of God concerning the realm you want to possess. These thoughts will give you strength and courage to possess it.

COMPREHENDING NEW REALMS OF LIVING

Because every realm has its own thoughts, often people can barely comprehend how much better the next level is than the one they are living on now. That's why it's so difficult to get people to move from one level of living to another. It is not in their thought life. If their minds cannot conceive it, they cannot receive it. Often a person does not see the possibilities or opportunities that are in front of him, especially if they are in another realm or level than what he is presently operating in.

It was difficult for the Israelites to possess the Promised Land because they had difficulty conceiving in their minds the benefits and privileges of going into another land.

On the other hand, David was a person who reminded himself of the benefits of serving God. *"Bless the Lord, O my soul, and forget not all his benefits"* (Psalms 103:2).

While Rev. Happy Caldwell was driving around the Hawaiian Islands, he drove by a large, fabulous mansion, and Rev. Caldwell commented, "I can't imagine living in a mansion like that." Immediately the Holy Spirit spoke up on the inside of him and said, *"Then you'll never have it."* Rev. Caldwell went on to say, *"You cannot possess what you cannot imagine."*[2]

Changing the thoughts in your mind to God's way of thinking means changing your lifestyle and way of doing things. Your entire approach to life will change. If you are willing to leave your old thoughts, God will elevate you to a new level of thinking and living.

REMOVING THE VEIL OF
BLINDNESS FROM YOUR MIND

Many people have a "veil of blindness" over their minds. Paul said concerning the Jews that there was a veil over their minds and that is why they could not recognize the Messiah.

Seeing then that we have such hope, we use great plainness of speech:

And not as Moses, which put a veil over his face, that the children of Israel could not steadfastly look to the end of that which is abolished:

But their minds were blinded; for until this day remaineth the same veil untaken away in the reading of the old testament; which veil is done away in Christ.

But even unto this day, when Moses is read, the veil is upon their heart.

Nevertheless when it shall turn to the Lord, the veil shall be taken away.

Now the Lord is that Spirit: and where the Spirit of the Lord is, there is liberty.

But we all, with open face beholding as in a glass the glory of the Lord, are changed into the same image from glory to glory, even as by the Spirit of the Lord.

(2 Corinthians 3:12-18)

Some people's minds have a veil of blindness concerning certain truths in the Word of God. Various things can cause people to be blinded to God's Word, including tradition, erroneous teaching, experiences in life, and sin. Satan himself blinds people's minds so they do not receive salvation (2 Corinthians 4:4).

The greatest liberty the Spirit of God will give you is to remove the veil of blindness from your mind and enable you to think God's thoughts in your mind. If this is to happen, you must read the Word and receive the change in your mind and heart by the power of the Holy Spirit. Ask the Holy Spirit to remove the veil from your understanding so you can comprehend what the Word of God is saying to you.

Soon after I became born again and found out God wanted me to prosper, I noticed that because of my upbringing, my mind would not comprehend financial terms or systems, understand investments, nor move in a realm of financial freedom. The church I grew up in believed that investments were wrong, especially the stock market and the commodity markets. We were not an extremely poor family, but we were not as well off as most of the people in our community, so these things made a strong impression upon my mind.

Every time I studied financial matters, I didn't seem to have any ability to understand these things. My mind seemed as if it were in a "fog," my understanding was dull and it seemed as if I could not break through that veil into what I wanted to know about financial things.

But I began to renew my mind with the Word of God concerning financial things. I found out what the Bible really says about finances, and how to operate in them. I began to see that God wanted me to have finances, and not to go through this life without money. Nowhere in the Word of God does it say God does not want us to have money.

Money in itself is neither good nor bad. Your motives about money and what you do with money determines whether it is good or evil. The Word of God states that the "love of money," not money itself, is the root of all evil. (**1 Timothy 6:10**).

As I continued to study the Word of God, and the financial system of this world, my mind gradually came out of the "fog" into a clear understanding. One day as I was in the presence of the Lord, I felt the Holy Ghost impress upon me that from this time forward I would understand financial systems. It has been a liberating experience to be able to understand financial things that I had not been able to understand before.

On another occasion when I was the Dean of a Bible school, I became very frustrated with the administrative duties. One day I told God, "Please find someone else to be the Dean. Just let me be an instructor, and I'll teach the Word, because I don't have the administrative abilities this job requires."

The Lord answered me and said, "I look at you as a good administrator." In that moment I realized God had equipped me to step into the role of administrator. Sometimes God has thoughts about you that differ from your own thoughts. *When the Holy Spirit reveals God's thoughts to you about yourself, you can step into the calling God has placed upon your life.*

For I know the thoughts that I think toward you, saith the Lord, thoughts of peace, and not of evil, to give you an expected end.
(Jeremiah 29:11)

Here God spoke to the Israelites through His prophet to reveal His thoughts to them. They had been deported from their homeland and made captives in Babylon because of their wickedness, disobedience, and idolatry.

Yet God stated His thoughts with them revealing how He looked upon them. He declared thoughts of peace toward them. God saw them with hearts turned toward Him, saying if they would seek Him, they would find Him. God promised restoration instead of total judgment.

Notice that God said He wanted to give the Israelites "...*an expected end.*" What does He mean by that? God wanted the outcome of the Israelites to be according to the promises He had made to them in His covenant with them.

God wants your end to be what His Word promises you. He expects the promises of His Word to be your outcome in life. Hallelujah! God has already mapped out a success plan for you in His Word. As you read the Word, realize God wants this to be the outcome of your life. The Word of God will unveil your future! As you follow the Word of God, your life will be one of peace and not evil, and you'll have a guaranteed outcome!

God's thoughts will lift you up to another level of living. Let the Holy Spirit remove the veil from your mind and reveal God's thoughts from His Word to you, because it will change your life.

RECEIVE THE SPIRIT OF WISDOM & REVELATION

(I) Cease not to give thanks for you, making mention of you in my prayers;

That the God of our Lord Jesus Christ, the Father of glory, may give unto you the spirit of wisdom and revelation in the knowledge of him:

The eyes of your understanding being enlightened; that ye may know what is the hope of his calling...

(Ephesians 1:16-18)

Most people are clueless about the will of God for their lives. It is a mystery to them. You need to pray for a spirit of wisdom and revelation so that your understanding is enlightened according to the will of God. **Psalms 18:28** tells us, *"For thou wilt light my candle: the Lord my God will enlighten my darkness."* God will enlighten you so that you are not in the dark concerning His will.

The Living Bible translated **Ephesians 1:18** this way, *"I pray that your heart will be flooded with light so that you can see something of the future he has called you to share..."* God wants to share His thoughts about your future with you. You can know what the Word of God tells you about your future, therefore your future does not have to be a mystery to you. Let God give you a revelation of His realm so you can know who He is, what He has, and what He wants for you. If you will seek God's face, He will begin to share His thoughts with you. The Holy Spirit will show you what is going to happen. **Jeremiah 33:3** instructs us to, *"Call unto me, and I will answer thee, and show thee great and mighty things, which thou knowest not."* Jesus also said in **John 16:13**, *"Howbeit when he, the Spirit of truth, is come, he will guide you into all truth: for he shall not speak of himself; but whatsoever he shall hear, that shall he speak: and he will show you things to come."* One thing the Holy Spirit does is reveal God's will to you.

Begin to pray Paul's prayer on a regular basis. *You will never be enlightened as to what the will of God is for your life without regular prayer.* Ask God for the spirit of revelation and wisdom to manifest in you. Pray that your heart will be flooded with light (knowledge) so that you may know His thoughts.

DON'T LOOK BACK TO THE PAST

Now the just shall live by faith: but if any man draw back, my soul shall have no pleasure in him.
But we are not of them who draw back unto perdition; but of them that believe to the saving of the soul.
(Hebrews 10:38-39)

The realms and dimensions of life God wants you to enter into are in front of you. Don't waste your time looking back; looking back will cause you to become a monument. That's what happened to Lot's wife when she looked back to the place they had left.

Looking forward gives you the anticipation and momentum you need to enter into the realms of life God has for you. Van Crouch said, *"There's no point in looking back unless that's the direction you want to go."*[3] Looking back is not an option when you are walking by faith.

Paul said in **Philippians 3:13,** *"Brethren, I count not myself to have apprehended: but his one thing I do, forgetting those things which are behind, and reaching forth unto those things which are before."* The word "forgetting" is from the Greek word *epilanthanomai* which means *to lose out of one's mind, or to neglect.* Choose to neglect the things of the past and focus on the future God has for you. Pastor Paul Zink said, *"What you feed grows, and what you starve dies."* Starve some old things of the past to death by neglecting the thoughts of them. Feed on new thoughts of the future God has for you.

JESUS HAS CONQUERED EVERY REALM

Wherefore he saith, When he ascended up on high, he led captivity captive, and gave gifts unto men.

(Now that he ascended, what is it but that he also descended first into the lower parts of the earth?

He that descended is the same also that ascended up far above all heavens, that he might fill all things."
(Ephesians 4:8-10)

Jesus has entered into every realm and established His Lordship. Everywhere Jesus went He conquered the opposition by winning them to His side, or by defeating them. When Adam gave up his right to be in charge of this earth and rule it for God, Satan had a right to establish his domain.

But Jesus came into the earth and took back all the devil had taken. Jesus has descended into the lowest realms, and ascended into the highest realms that exist.

Jesus made a way for you to enter into every realm, dimension, and level of life to which He has called you. There is no realm that you cannot go to at the direction of God. You have a legal right to be there because Jesus has gone before you. Now you can boldly possess the land and live in the realms of God here on earth.

God has given you the equipment necessary to enter into the realms of life He has promised you in His Word. He has given you (1) the Word of God (2) the Name of Jesus (3) the blood of Jesus (4) the anointing and power of the Holy Spirit (5) the whole armor of God and (6) faith in His Word. You must use this equipment if you're going to enter into new realms of life. However, if you don't have the right mind-set, or right thinking, you will not use the equipment God has given to you to enter into what He has promised.

It is possible for you to live on a higher level than you do right now. Begin to think the thoughts of God's Word and you will begin to see a whole new world opening up to you. Your horizons will be enlarged: new possibilities and opportunities will come to you! New lands are waiting for you to possess them!

POINTS TO PONDER

1. EVERY REALM HAS ITS OWN THOUGHTS.

2. THE GREATEST LIBERTY THE SPIRIT OF GOD WILL GIVE YOU IS IN REMOVING THE VEIL OF BLINDNESS FROM YOUR MIND AND ENABLING YOU TO THINK GOD'S THOUGHTS IN YOUR MIND.

3. "THERE'S NO POINT IN LOOKING BACK UNLESS THAT'S THE DIRECTION YOU WANT TO GO." (VAN CROUCH)

4. JESUS MADE A WAY FOR YOU TO ENTER INTO EVERY REALM, DIMENSION, AND LEVEL OF LIFE TO WHICH HE HAS CALLED YOU.

Chapter 14

THOUGHTS FOR INCREASE

LIVING IN THE LAND OF MORE THAN ENOUGH

"God wants His children to move out of the land of not enough, through the land of just enough, into the land of more than enough."[1] (Mark Hankins). Supernatural increase is the will of God for His children.

Jesus said in **John 10:10,** *"...I am come that they might have life, and that they might have it more abundantly."* God does not want us to live below what He has promised in His Word. Jesus died on the cross so that you and I could have ALL the promises in God's Word **(2 Corinthians 1:20)**.

Some people act as if their request would bankrupt God. Listen, God is the one who made it all **(Colossians 1:16)**. God has it all. If He doesn't have what you requested He can make it for you!

Oral Roberts said, *"There is no shortage of God's resources, friend; none whatsoever. There is only a shortage of faith, and in our understanding of the goodness of God."*[2] You must enlarge your thoughts to encompass who God really is, what He has, and what He wants to do for His children.

Where you live is a choice you make daily: in the land of not enough, the land of just enough, or in the land of more than enough. *"Every day you make a choice: either you exercise faith and feast in the abundance of God's supply, or you give in to the devil and fear and suffer personal famine."*[3] (John Avanzini).

Wealth & Increase Are Available

There is plenty of wealth in the earth for everyone. Think of all the minerals, precious metals, natural resources, and all that the earth is able to produce for the benefit of mankind. Some people would have you believe that we are about to exhaust the resources in the earth. But God did not miscalculate when He created the earth and the wealth in it!

However, there is a lot of wealth in the earth that man has not even found yet. Recently I watched a documentary of how man is exploring the bottom of the ocean, which was referred to as "The Last Frontier." Depicted were some of the things man has developed in order to explore the deepest parts of the ocean. There is more of the surface of the earth under water than on dry land. There are vast riches in these regions that have yet to be discovered and put into use for the benefit of mankind.

In the book THE MILLIONAIRE NEXT DOOR,[4] it is stated that in 1996 there were over 22 trillion dollars in American households. The problem of increase is not a lack of resources. *However, we must know how to appropriate that wealth and increase into our lives.* This book went on to say that over half of the 22 trillion dollars is in the hands of 3.5% of Americans. This simply shows that most people don't know how to get their share of available wealth.

As Christians, we are members of the most affluent family in the universe – the family of God. God is the creator of all wealth in the earth, and as His children, we are entitled to it. We are the ones for whom God created it in the first place – not the devil and his bunch. Norman Vincent Peale said, *"There seems to be an invisible reservoir of abundance in the universe that can be tapped into by obeying certain spiritual laws."*[5]

You must become aware of the wealth and increase available to you before you can have it. As a Christian who wants to obey

God, you also need to believe God wants you to have wealth and increase. You are the reason God put all this wealth in the earth.

GETTING READY FOR
SUPERNATURAL INCREASE

Enlarge the place of thy tent, and let them stretch forth the curtains of thine habitations: spare not, lengthen thy cords, and strengthen thy stakes;
For thou shalt break forth on the right hand and on the left: and thy seed shall inherit the gentiles, and make the desolate cities to be inhabited.

(Isaiah 54:2-3)

In these verses God shares how to prepare for the increase He wants you to have. Increase will be a blessing and not a curse to you if you prepare for it. The different phrases used here reveal how to get ready for the increase God wants to bring to you.

"Enlarge the place of thy tent." The word "enlarge" means *to broaden and make room in the condition of your mind and body.* Enlarge your mind to embrace the thoughts of God and the work He wants to do in your life and ministry. You will be able to receive increase and prosperity as you renew your mind with God's thoughts from His Word.

"Stretch forth the curtains of thine habitations." Habitations are where you have a habit of being. Move outside your comfort zone. Go to places that will enlarge your thinking. Get around people who have dared to attempt things that seemed impossible. Change the places you go habitually, and go to places that will lift you to a higher level of thinking, vision, and performance.

"Spare not." This means *do not refrain, withhold, or reserve your imagination and efforts.* Use every resource you

have to get ready for increase. Use your thoughts and imaginations to meditate upon the possibililties of God's Word coming to pass in your life. Work hard to press toward the promises of God's Word.

"Lengthen thy cords." You're to *draw out, prolong, and lengthen* your thoughts. For example, a dog tied to a post with a cord will be limited in his activities, resources, and provision. The resources the dog needs may be just beyond the length of the cord he is tied to but he can't reach it. Therefore he is limited in what he can experience in life.

Thoughts are the links in the chains that determine your level of existence and achievements in life. You are either limited by your thoughts so you can't have what you desire, or your thoughts are large enough to allow you to reach the goals and the potential to which God has called you. Shakespeare said, *"Make not your thoughts your prison."*[6]

Open your mind to what God said in His Word that He has for His children. T. L. Osborne said, *"When the mind perceives God's abundance and begins to comprehend that He created the wealth of this earth for the blessing of His children, the walls of mental enslavement begin to crumble and the rainbow of God's plenty appears."*[7]

"Strengthen thy stakes." You must be courageous, conquering, established, and prevailing in your thought life. Otherwise you will not be strong enough to take a stand and see the Word of God come to pass. Fortify your mind with the Word of God and continue until you see the increase God has promised. Persist in building Bible-based attitudes until your mind becomes a castle that won't be moved away from the Word of God.

Satan will cause adversity to come to you. Don't be moved away from what God is saying to you. Satan wants to steal the

Word of God out of your life so you have nothing left to stand on. *"If Satan can capture your thought life, he has won a great victory"*[8] (Mark Hankins).

Continue daily to feed upon the Word of God until your mind and heart are firmly established with God's thoughts. Never let up on your spiritual progress. Then Satan cannot find a foothold to enter into your life, and you will maintain the victory that belongs to you according to God's Word.

Prepare for the increase God has promised to you in His Word, and you will begin to break forth on every hand. The things that were desolate and barren and did not produce will flourish and bring forth abundance. People will ask you what happened, and you will be able to say, "The Lord did this for me, and if you obey His Word, He will do it for you too!"

GROWING INTO
THE THINGS OF GOD

Learn to grow yourself into the things of God. Sometimes I tell my wife, "Let's grow ourselves into what God is saying." By this I mean we are going to change the condition of our souls which will enable us to experience what God has told us. How do you grow yourself into what God has for you?

First, I search the Word for scriptures that apply to the areas I need to grow in. I continually read and meditate upon these scriptures until they become a part of me. They show up in my talk and in my walk. I feed on these scriptures until I'm bubbling over with scriptures that declare a successful outcome in my situation. **Luke 6:45b** tells us that, *"...out of the abundance of the heart the mouth speaketh."* I keep taking the scriptures in until there is an abundance in me.

I also find people with teaching on the areas that I am dealing with, and I read their books and listen to their tapes. I make sure that my spiritual and mental diet reflects the realm where I want to go and what I want to accomplish, so I can fulfill the call of God upon my life.

If it's possible to do so, I find people who have already gone through what I am going through to see what they did to have a successful outcome. These people can share wisdom from their experiences that will save you many steps and hours of labor. The reason the different incidents of the Israelites and other people in the Bible were recorded was to enable us to learn from them **(1 Corinthians 10:11)**.

During this time of growing I listen to the Holy Spirit to see what He has to say about my situation. He sees and knows all things. He is able to guide me into the perfect will of God. I watch for a scripture that the Holy Spirit may quicken to my spirit to use as a guiding sign of (1) what *He* wants to do, and (2) what He wants *me* to do.

I go to meetings where the glory of God is being manifested. There I am able to change my thoughts, receive God's thoughts, and embrace the changes God wants me to make with the least amount of resistance.

The glory of God is invaluable in changing your thought life. It gets you out beyond the level of thinking you have had before and frees you to think higher thoughts.

Where you grow yourself into the things of God by changing the condition of your soul, you develop the right mind-set to operate in the other things the Word of God tells you to do. You can pray according to God's will, exercise strong faith in His Word, and operate in the laws of sowing and reaping. You can move in the anointing and flow with the Holy Ghost as He ministers in the earth, and become a channel through which God's miraculous power flows.

Some people are waiting for God's miraculous power to move suddenly to deliver them. Many people need God to move suddenly for them. If God doesn't do miracles for them, they have no answers.

However, unless you prepare yourself to receive God's miracles by renewing your mind to His thoughts and ways, you may not be in a position to know, recognize, or to receive what He is doing.

Beloved, I wish above all things that thou mayest prosper and be in health, even as thy soul prospereth.
(3 John 2)

It starts when you change the condition of your soul. Remember the equation in **3 John 2** that goes like this:

YOUR HEALTH & PROSPERITY ARE EQUAL TO THE CONDITION OF YOUR SOUL

Sometimes you need to wait upon God to get direction or anointing. There are times when you need God to perform a miracle for you because nothing else will supply what you need. But often you can simply grow yourself into the things of God by changing the condition of your soul. As you do so, God will bless you with all He has promised you in His Word.

I believe many Christians do not receive the inheritance they are entitled to according to the Word of God because they never grow up. Babies, children, and even teenagers cannot correctly deal with large amounts of wealth or increase. They will either spend it all in a short period of time or ruin their lives by purchasing things that are detrimental to them. In fact, the inheritance God had meant for a blessing could be the very thing that the devil would use to ruin their lives unless they have grown up and matured in the Lord.

I heard the story of a very wealthy couple who found out they could not have any children. However, they kept believing God's Word, and finally in their later years they did have a child. One day after the child was several years old, the father lifted the child up and said, *"I can't wait for you to grow up so I can show you my world!"*

God wants His children to grow up so He can show them His world. He desires to give what He has to His children. He wants to see His children blessed! *Today is not a life sentence with God! God wants you to move on up!*

POINTS TO PONDER

1. SUPERNATURAL INCREASE IS THE WILL OF GOD FOR HIS CHILDREN.

2. THOUGHTS ARE THE LINKS IN THE CHAINS THAT DETERMINE OUR LIFE'S EXISTENCE AND ACHIEVEMENTS.

3. YOUR HEALTH AND YOUR PROSPERITY ARE EQUAL TO THE CONDITION OF YOUR SOUL.

4. GOD WANTS HIS CHILDREN TO GROW UP SO HE CAN SHOW THEM HIS WORLD.

CHAPTER ONE
1. Jack Hartman, TRUST GOD FOR YOUR FINANCES, p. 43
2. Gloria Copeland, GOD'S WILL IS PROSPERITY, p. 35
3. T. D. Jakes, quoted in POWER TO GET WEALTH, by L. Blackwell, p. 8
4. John G. Lake, THE NEW JOHN G. LAKE SERMONS, p. 5
5. Dr. S. I. McMillan, NONE OF THESE DISEASES, p. 5
6. R. W. Emerson, quote from GOD'S PSYCHIATRY, by C. Allen, p. 15
7. Norman Vincent Peale, quote from GOD'S PSYCHIATRY, by C. Allen, p. 15
8. John Osteen, PULLING DOWN STRONGHOLDS, p. 32
9. Bob Harrison, story from FINANCIAL INCREASE tape series
10. John Maxwell, YOU CAN'T BE A SMART COOKIE..., p.p. 82, 102
11. Zig Ziglar, SEE YOU AT THE TOP, p.p. 202, 203
12. Bob Harrison, quote from FINANCIAL INCREASE tape series
13. Oliver Wendall Holmes, quoted in STEPS TO THE TOP, by Zig Ziglar, p. 152

CHAPTER TWO
1. Jerry Savelle, PROSPERITY OF THE SOUL, p. 34
2. Jerry Savelle, PROSPERITY OF THE SOUL, p. 55
3. St. Augustine, quote from GOD'S PSYCHIATRY, by C. Allen, p. 9
4. Horatio Spafford, HYMNS OF GLORIOUS PRAISE, #316
5. John Greenleaf Whittier, quote from GOD'S PSYCHIATRY, by C. Allen p. 19
6. The Scribner Bantam English Dictionary, © 1979, 1977 by Bantam Books, Inc.
7. John Dryden, quoted in SUPERSELF, by C.Givens, p. 141
8. R. W. Emerson, quote from THE HOME BOOK OF QUOTATIONS, p. 1992

CHAPTER THREE
1. James Allen, AS A MAN THINKETH, p. 19
2. Dr. Lester Sumrall, OVERCOMING COMPULSIVE DESIRES, p.56
3. Victor E. Frankl, MAN'S SEARCH FOR MEANING, p. 104
4. Helen McInnes, HORIZONS, p. 7
5. Alexander Dumas, quote from CONQUERING AN ENEMY CALLED AVERAGE, J. Mason, p. 42
6. Dr. Frank Crand, quote from CONQUERING AN ENEMY CALLED AVERAGE, J. Mason, p. 42
7. Booker T. Washington, quoted in SEE YOU AT THE TOP, Zig Ziglar, p. 73
8. Charles Allen, GOD'S PSYCHIATRY, p. 23
9. Zig Ziglar, SEE YOU AT THE TOP, p. 63

CHAPTER FOUR
1. Harold Hill, HOW TO FLIP YOUR FLAB FOREVER, p. 36
2. Mark Hankins, PIONEERS, SETTLERS, & MUSEUM KEEPERS tape series
3. Mark Hankins, PIONEERS, SETTLERS, & MUSEUM KEEPERS tape series

CHAPTER FIVE
1. C. "Tremendous" Jones, FINANCIAL INCREASE tape series, B. Harrison
2. Mike Murdock, THE WINNER'S DEVOTIONAL, p. 9
3. Mike Murdock, SEEDS OF WISDOM, p. 2
4. Bob Harrison, quote from FINANCIAL INCREASE tape series

CHAPTER SIX
1. Jerry Savelle, PROSPERITY OF THE SOUL, p. 34
2. John G. Lake, HIS LIFE, SERMONS, BOLDNESS OF FAITH, p. 88

CHAPTER SEVEN
1. Billy Joe Daugherty, THE GOAL, p. 23
2. Peter J. Daniels, HOW TO REACH YOUR LIFE GOALS, p. 20

CHAPTER EIGHT
1. Jerry Savelle, PROSPERITY OF THE SOUL, p. 34
2. Dale Carnegie, DALE CARNEGIE'S SCRAPBOOK, p. 165
3. Mark Hankins, PIONEERS, SETTLERS, & MUSEUM KEEPERS tape series
4. Successories
5. Charles Allen, GOD'S PSYCHIATRY, p.p. 145, 23

CHAPTER NINE
1. Robert Schuller, POWER THOUGHTS, p.p. 165, 166
2. David Seamonds, HEALING FOR DAMAGED EMOTIONS,
   p.p. 21, 22, 29, 32, 35

CHAPTER ELEVEN
1. Mark Hankins, PIONEERS, SETTLERS, & MUSEUM KEEPERS tape series
2. Bob Harrison, quote from CONQUERING AND ENEMY CALLED
   AVERAGE, by John Mason, p. 42
3. Stanley Jones, from IT'S JUST A THOUGHT..., by J. Maxwell, p. 114

CHAPTER TWELVE
1. Kenneth E. Hagin, RIGHT & WRONG THINKING, p. 2
2. E. W. Kenyon, THE TWO KINDS OF KNOWLEDGE, p.p. 33, 34
3. Kenneth E. Hagin, RIGHT & WRONG THINKING, p.p. 1, 2

CHAPTER THIRTEEN
1. Rev. Gerald Brooks, quote from COURAGE TO BE A LEADER cassette tape
2. Rev. Happy Caldwell, from a message preached at the WMF Convention
3. Van Crouch, STAYING IN THE GAME, p. 96

CHAPTER FOURTEEN
1. Mark Hankins, PIONEERS, SETTLERS, & MUSEUM KEEPERS tape series
2. Oral Roberts, THE MIRACLE OF SEED FAITH, p. 42
3. John Avanzini, ALWAYS ABOUNDING, p. 16
4. T. J. Stanley, & W. D. Danko, THE MILLIONAIRE NEXT DOOR, p. 2
5. Norman Vincent Peale, THE POWER OF POSITIVE THINKING
6. William Shakespeare, from THE HOME BOOK OF QUOTATIONS, p. 1996
7. T. L. Osborne, HOW TO ENJOY PLENTY, p. 16
8. Mark Hankins, PIONEERS, SETTLERS, & MUSEUM KEEPERS tape series

INTRODUCING MARVIN YODER

Marvin Yoder grew up in the Old Order Amish Church, driving a horse and buggy, having no car, radio, or television in his home. It is an exciting story of how God revealed himself to a 10-year-old Amish boy, and caused him to travel a path ordained by God.

As a teenager, Marvin ran away from home and became a pool hustler. But God revealed himself to Marvin again, saving him, delivering him, and healing him of many physical ailments.

Marvin is a 1984 graduate of Rhema Bible Training Center in Tulsa, Oklahoma. Since then he has pastored several churches in Kansas and Illinois. He has also served as the Dean of Christian Training Institute in central Illinois.

MARVIN YODER MINISTRIES
P.O. BOX 168, STONINGTON, IL 62567

BOOKS & STUDY GUIDES

The Traveling Minister's Handbook

Establishing New Ministries

The Teaching Ministry

Helps In The Church

Knowing The Spirit Of God

Following The Spirit Of God

Divine Healing

CASSETTE TAPE SERIES

Supernatural Increase

Helps Ministry In The Church

The Spirit-Filled Life

Following The Spirit Of God

Knowing The Spirit Of God

How To Flow With The Spirit Of God

Discovering The Will Of God

Divine Healing

Breaking Controlling Powers

The Journey Of Excellence

WORD OF LIFE SEMINARS

Marvin conducts Word of Life Seminars throughout the United States. These seminars are designed to build up, refresh, and motivate the Body of Christ. Seminar subjects include:

- **Maximizing Your Personal Growth**
- **The Journey Of Excellence**
- **Maximizing Your Leadership Skills**
- **Realities Of The Soul**
- **Helps Ministry In The Church**
- **Knowing The Holy Spirit**
- **Following The Spirit Of God**

You will be blessed by Marvin's practical, but often humorous presentation of God's Word! The Holy Spirit confirms the Word of God shared in Marvin's meetings with healings, miracles, and the gifts of the Spirit.

For more information about Word of Life Seminars, or to schedule a seminar or a speaking engagement please contact

Marvin Yoder Ministries

"Marvin recently ministered in our church, and it was so refreshing that I want to recommend him to you. Each service had excellent ministry, and the flow of the Holy Spirit was very precious."
Pastor Greg Roe, World Harvest Church, Springfield, IL

PRAYER TO
RECEIVE SALVATION

The greatest gift you could ever receive from God is the salvation of your soul. If you desire to receive forgiveness of your sins and make Jesus Christ the Lord of your life, please pray this prayer from your heart:

"Heavenly Father, your Word says *"whosoever shall call upon the Name of the Lord shall be saved"* (Romans 10:13). I call upon you today, I ask Jesus to become my Lord and Savior according to **Romans 10:9-19**, *"That if thou shalt confess with thy mouth the Lord Jesus, and shalt believe in thine heart that God hath raised him from the dead, thou shalt be saved. For with the heart man believeth unto righteousness; and with the mouth confession is made unto salvation."* I confess Jesus as my Lord and believe with my heart that God has raised Him from the dead.

Please forgive me of all my sins. Thank you for the blood of Jesus washing me clean and pure and making me righteous in Christ.

I am now a Christian. I am born again. I am a child of God. Thank you, Father, for receiving me into the family of God. Amen."